Youth Unemployment:

Why inequality matters and how to promote equality

Xiaolong Hou

Copyright © 2019 Xiaolong Hou

All rights reserved.

ISBN: 978-1-675-71381-5

Table of Contents

ACKNOWLEDGMENTS III
PREFACE: THE NECESSITY OF LEARNING MORE ABOUT YOUTH UNEMPLOYMENT 1

PART A: THE YOUTH UNEMPLOYMENT PROBLEM 7

1. YOUTH UNEMPLOYMENT PROBLEM: INTRODUCTION 9
   1.1 Definition of youth unemployment 9
   1.2 The latest youth unemployment crisis 10
   1.3 The harm of youth unemployment for the public 13
   1.4 One representative of current solutions: Youth Guarantee 15
   1.5 Characteristics and rationalities of current solutions 16
2. TO EXPLORE MORE ABOUT YOUTH UNEMPLOYMENT 19
   2.1 Outcome and worries of current solutions 19
   2.2 Puzzles about the reason of youth unemployment 22
   2.3 Historical youth unemployment rate 27
   2.4 Financial crisis and youth unemployment crisis 32
   2.5 Shortcomings of "Youth Unemployment Rate" 35
   2.6 To warm-up: new question arises as more facts being examined 38
3. LABOR-SUPPLY PERSPECTIVE OF YOUTH UNEMPLOYMENT ANALYSIS 43
   3.1 Two perspectives of analyzing youth unemployment problem 43
   3.2 Lack of skills also matters 46
   3.3 One-stakeholder approach of youth unemployment analysis 48
   3.4 The necessities of one-stakeholder analysis (1) 52
   3.5 The necessities of one-stakeholder analysis (2) 55
   3.6 The focus and assumptions of my analysis 60

PART B: THE ANALYSIS OF YOUTH UNEMPLOYMENT PROBLEM 65

4. THE RECRUITMENT FORMULA 67
   4.1 Recruitment: the starting point of understanding youth
   unemployment 67
   4.2 Recruitment Formula: definition 69
   4.3 Benefits and costs of recruitment 72
   4.4 The X-factor 76
   4.5 Long-term concern of recruitment 80
   4.6 Formula implementation: understanding more facts about
   labor-supply (1) 82
   4.7 Formula implementation: understanding more facts about
   labor-supply (2) 87
5. YOUTH UNEMPLOYMENT AND WEALTH INEQUALITY 93
   5.1 A further exploration of reasons behind youth unemployment 93
   5.2 Wealth matters 96
   5.3 Information matters 99
   5.4 Wealth, information and youth unemployment 101
   5.5 Sources of wealth and information 104
   5.6 Family: another stakeholder in youth unemployment analysis 109
   5.7 Consistency between the possession of wealth and information 111
   5.8 Youth unemployment and wealth inequality 114
   5.9 Issues concerning the relationship between wealth and
   unemployment 121
6. INFORMATION ASYMMETRY, SIGNALS AND THE DIMENSION OF TIME 125

6.1 Trace backwards into the past 125
6.2 Possessing university degree shows positive signal for recruiters .. 127
6.3 Information asymmetry and the role of signals 128
6.4 Signals and youth unemployment 130
6.5 A brief clarification about signals 133
6.6 The formation of signals 136
6.7 The logic of youth unemployment problem 138
6.8 One serious yet neglected social problem 140

PART C: THE SOLUTION OF YOUTH UNEMPLOYMENT PROBLEM................... 145

7. INFORMATION EQUALITY IS THE KEY.. 147
   7.1 Elaboration of solutions 147
   7.2 The role of information 148
   7.3 The interaction between information and wealth 149
   7.4 The inequality of information 152
   7.5 The transferability of information 154
   7.6 Three questions about promoting information equality 157
8. THE INFORMATION NEEDED.. 159
   8.1 A multi-stakeholder issue in nature 159
   8.2 Who also need information 160
   8.3 Information needed for the youth (1) 163
   8.4 Information needed for the youth (2) 166
   8.5 Information needed for other stakeholders 170
   8.6 The society's strategy 172
9. CAREER INFORMATION CENTER.. 177
   9.1 Arrangement of promoting information equality 177
   9.2 Implementation: career information center 178
   9.3 Career Information Center and Education system 180
   9.4 Other concerns relating to career information center 183
   9.5 Career information center and the arrangement for today's
        unemployed youths 186
10. EXTENDED DISCUSSIONS 189
    10.1 Three guidelines for young people 189
    10.2 Strategies for young people 191
    10.3 Keep investing in yourself and keep learning 193
    10.4 A new angle of understanding wealth inequality 195
    10.5 The opportunity behind youth unemployment crisis 198

THE CONCLUSION 201
AFTERWORD 205
ABOUT THE AUTHOR.. 207
BIBLIOGRAPHY.. 209

ACKNOWLEDGMENTS

Youth unemployment issue is relatively a new topic and there is little data except for "youth unemployment rate", a fact that has made it difficult to conduct analysis. Here before the start of my book, I want to express my sincere gratitude to McKinsey Center for Government for their global surveys and two reports on youth unemployment problem.

If McKinsey doesn't issue the report *Education to Employment: Designing A System that Works*, I will certainly not be able to write this book, since the report not only presents hard data showing that a lack of skills is also the cause of youth unemployment problem, which makes me confident enough to follow my intuition and go on my research, but also helps when I carefully read contents of the report, which encourages me to reorganize many of my ideas.

As readers will find in my book, data and facts in their reports—derived from results of their global surveys, provide the foundation of my discussions, and it is proper to say that if they do not publish these two reports, I won't be able to finish this book.

McKinsey, thanks

PREFACE: THE NECESSITY OF LEARNING MORE ABOUT YOUTH UNEMPLOYMENT

During my gathering information on youth unemployment in the end of 2013, I was surprised to find that macroeconomic situation—a weakened economy following the latest global financial crisis, had been taken as the main cause of the sudden rising of youth unemployment rate. The core idea behind this belief was that the weak economy had greatly reduced the amount of job opportunities available for the youth and young people could not find jobs simply because there were not enough job positions opening. As a result, almost all the attention of policy makers has focused on how to create more job positions to accommodate the large number of unemployed youths.

There are rationalities behind this belief. As is shown in figure 1, youth unemployment rate for the world as a whole rose from 12.5% in 2007 to 12.9% in 2008 and rose once again to 13.7% in 2009, a pattern that matched the evolvement of financial crisis. It is true that weak demand lead by a weak economy will cut off production, and as companies reduce their demand for labor, more people, including the youth, will find it more difficult to get jobs and thus tend to be unemployed. Besides, as having been extensively addressed in many researches, failing to obtain a job in younger age may have adverse effect in the long run, such as higher risk of falling into long-term unemployment compared with those who have jobs at an early age, and the longer this unemployment period lasts, the worse the possible future effect would be[1].

As a result, to help those unemployed youth and prevent them from falling into long-term unemployment, there is an urgent need to provide them with jobs or trainings. For this purpose, European Union has carried out a project named as Youth Guarantee, which aims to mobilize around €45 billion during 2014 and 2015, to provide every young people under 25 a proper job or traineeship within four months of leaving school or losing their jobs[2,3].

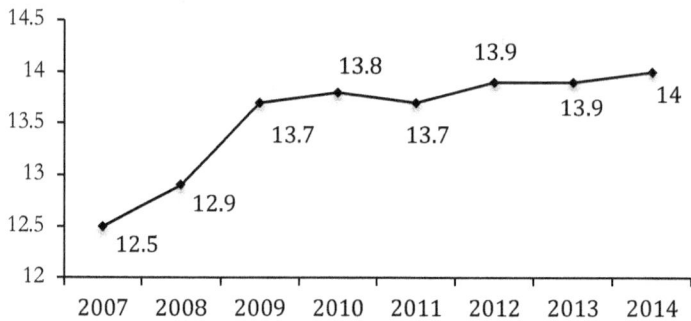

Figure 1 Youth unemployment rate of the world overall

Source: World Bank[4]

While the motivation of setting up mechanisms to provide jobs to those unemployed youth is justified, and these mechanisms are supported by economic theories, we still need to think more, to think beyond the current situation of youth unemployment problem. Suppose these efforts that aim to create jobs for the youth, such as the Youth Guarantee project, are implemented successfully without the need to worry for funding cost or other issues, and suppose those projects achieve their predetermined goals—thus youth unemployment rate falls significantly after their carrying out, there's still a need to look beyond current youth unemployment situation and ask, whether our methods will help to ease potential youth unemployment problem in the future, rather than just existing as a temporary expedient. To examine youth unemployment problem from a long-term point of view and prevent it from recurring is of necessity, since each country, or our human society as a whole, may be able to cope with youth unemployment crisis occurred each time, but for specific individuals, they are vulnerable and are less likely to deal with unemployment crisis—the consequence of which for individuals might be destructive.

Figure 2 exhibits the world's historical youth unemployment rates with a longer time horizon, starting from 1991. It shows clearly that youth unemployment rate has once been higher than it is now, which means that this is not the first time that youth unemployment crisis bursts out. Just as I have mentioned, we do need to explore more about the causes of youth unemployment problem, especially from a long-term view.

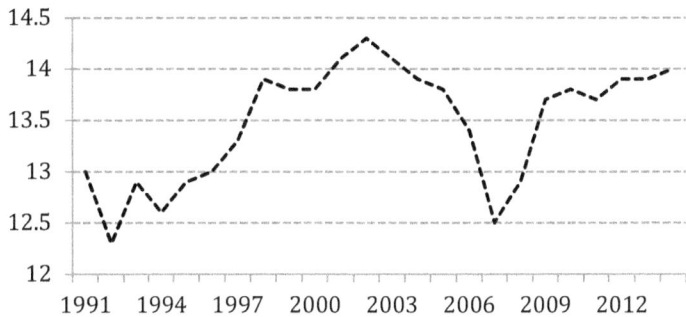

Figure 2 Youth unemployment rate of the world

Source: World Bank[5]

To answer the question that whether our efforts currently carried out will help conquer youth unemployment problem, or in other words, whether our efforts to create job positions now will prevent youth unemployment problem from recurring in the future, we need to examine and testify carefully the relationship between jobs opportunities and youth unemployment problem, rather than just relying on the short-term fact that today's unemployed youth need jobs.

The rise of unemployment rate has been traditionally considered as a sign of decline of economy, a belief that one paperwork[6] has made it quite straightforward by saying that unemployment rate measures the economy's ability to generate employment and reflects its ability to absorb labor force. As a result, to enhance employment, government should take actions to boost economy so as to create more job positions available for the public. Currently, this school of thought that is dominating in the analysis of **unemployment** issue has also been applied to the analysis of **youth unemployment**.

While this helps, we have to acknowledge that compared with a generalized unemployment issue, youth unemployment is relatively a new topic, and it is possible that we cannot simply apply the framework used to analyze unemployment to the analysis of youth unemployment.

The necessity of learning more about youth unemployment

This is true when we realize that there are significant differences between young people and older people, especially concerning situations that they are faced with. For example, young people tend to be more idealistic and they have less life burden on their shoulder, and as a result, they are more likely to turn down "ordinary" jobs and look forward to "great" ones—a phenomenon that tends to drive up youth unemployment rate. This means the explanation power of reduced number of job positions falls when it comes to discuss youth unemployment, and in order to analyze youth unemployment problem, we need a new framework.

When we follow the traditional logic that the rise of youth unemployment rate reflects a weakening of the economy's ability to create jobs—thus to lower youth unemployment rate we must provide more jobs to the youth, we inherently hold the assumption that young people are properly qualified for employment and they are competent enough to take up almost all jobs available for them. But is this assumption sound? Is it true that the rising of youth unemployment rate is solely due to a lack of job opportunities and has nothing to do with the competencies of the youth?

This is a key question for the purpose of analyzing youth unemployment problem and it derives relatively from the perspective of labor-supply. While few researches were conducted based on this aspect before, many do emerge during this latest youth unemployment crisis and researchers have noticed that the competencies of young people also matter much. For example, McKinsey, a management consulting company with worldwide reputation, has conducted a global survey from 2011 to 2012, targeting at the confusing phenomenon that while large amount of youth couldn't find jobs, there are also plenty of companies couldn't find enough skilled entry-level workers.

McKinsey's global survey covers 4,500 youth, 2,700 employers and 900 education providers across 9 countries[i], the result of which is exhibited collectively in its report issued in 2012: *Education to Employment: Designing A System that Works*[7]. Based on the result of its global survey, it states that there is a significant number of unfilled entry-level job positions existing and the average number for large, medium and small[ii] companies are 27, 13 and 3 respectively[8]. What's more, almost 40% employers respond that a lack of skills is one core reason for this

---

[i] Brazil, Germany, India, Mexico, Morocco, Saudi Arabia, Turkey, UK and US.
[ii] According to this report, companies are considered as small when their employees are less than 50, medium when their employees range from 50 to 500, and large when they have more than 500 employees

entry-level job vacancies[9].

Based on results of the global survey conducted by McKinsey, we could find that the traditional assumption that the rise of youth unemployment rate reflects a weakening of the economy's ability to create jobs may not always hold, which means that many young people are, in fact, not competent enough—at least believed by some employers—to take up job positions that are available for them. As a result, rather than analyzing youth unemployment problem solely from the aspect of labor demand, which focuses on the relationship between the number of job positions and the number of job seekers, there is also a need to conduct research from the aspect of labor supply, which relates to the competencies of young people. That is to say, in order to get a comprehensive view of youth unemployment problem and to propose effective solutions to tackle it, there is a need to find more clues from the youth.

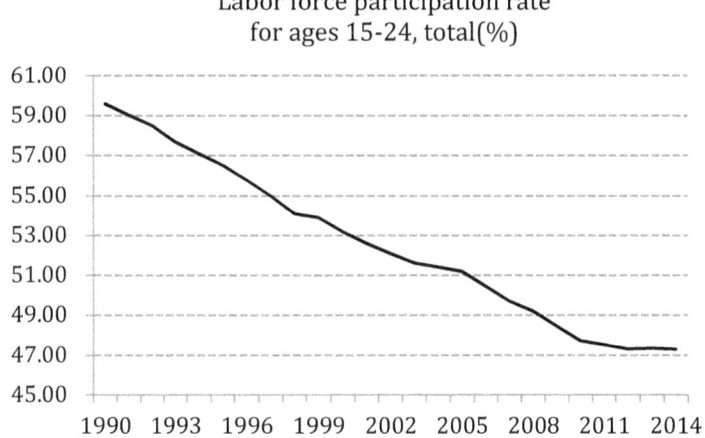

Figure 3 Labor force participation rate of the world

Source: World Bank[10]

This is especially essential when we realize that youth unemployment rate is never a perfect indicator of the employment situation that youth people are faced with. And when we examine other set of figures, we could find valuable information from other dimensions. Figure 3 exhibits young people's labor participation rate for the world, which shows an on-going declining trend, and this is much worrying than the situation reflected by the fluctuation of youth unemployment rate during the same period.

Different from youth unemployment rate, labor force participation rate for young people takes those who don't belong to the labor force into consideration, and thus is a more comprehensive indicator. To our surprise, the fact that labor force participation rate shows is even more worrisome than that exhibited by youth unemployment rate, and this strengthens our determination to search for more clues from young people.

The purpose of this book is to turn people's attention from labor demand to labor supply and to analyze causes as well as solutions of youth unemployment problem through a thorough and in-depth analysis of youth people. I hope this book could perform as a supplement to our current knowledge, to help build a comprehensive understanding of youth unemployment and finally, to try to prevent youth unemployment crisis from recurring in the future.

To conclude, this book focuses less on the current youth unemployment situation but discusses exhaustively from the perspective of labor supply—thus the youth. I hope this book will help enrich people's knowledge about youth unemployment, for which I have devoted several years of hard work. I would be greatly satisfied if there are readers who find this book interesting and somewhat helpful and have the interests to move forward to analyze youth unemployment problem from the perspective of labor supply.

Part A: The youth unemployment problem

1. YOUTH UNEMPLOYMENT PROBLEM: INTRODUCTION

1.1 Definition of youth unemployment

The growth rate of economy[i], unemployment rate and inflation rate are three key figures that drive government's economic policies, which we would notice every day and everywhere. For unemployment rate, it matters because it indicates the number of people who do not have a job but seek one. When the number of people having no jobs rises above a certain level, as is shown by a relatively high unemployment rate, the economy is considered to be weak and needs government's action, to prevent it from getting worse.

The commonly used "unemployment rate" measures the employment situation of total labor force that constitutes of people from various age groups. Different from it, "youth unemployment rate" specifically focuses on the employment situation of young people, typically aged between 15 and 24. According to the ILO, youth unemployment rate indicates the amount of unemployed young people, which consists of those that aged between 15 and 24, have no work but are able to work and are actively seeking work, and it is calculated by dividing the number of unemployed youth by total youth labor force.

$$Youth\ Unemployment\ Rate = \frac{number\ of\ unemployed\ young\ persons}{Youth\ Labor\ Force}$$

Source: The Youth Employment Network, ILO.

Concerning the definition and calculation of youth unemployment rate, two things need to be stressed here:

Firstly, youth unemployment rate measures the employment situation of people aged between 15 and 24, and people from other age groups, whether younger than 15 or older than 24, will not be included in the

---

[i] Typically measured by GDP, gross domestic product

calculation of youth unemployment rate. As will be revealed later in this book, age issue is important to the analysis of youth unemployment, not only because people within this age range have certain characteristics but also because life in this stage is very different from that of other stages.

Secondly, youth labor force (over a specific period) equals the number of young people aged between 15 and 24 who are employed plus that of those who are unemployed. Since many young people within this age range still study at school and are not considered as unemployed even though they don't have jobs, this group of youth who study at school is often presumably excluded in the analysis of youth unemployment simply because they don't belong to youth labor force. However, we try to analyze the unemployment issue of young people doesn't necessarily mean we just examine the group of people who belong to youth labor force, since whether seeking for employment or being at study are just two different status of people within that age group, and to include those study at school in the analysis of youth unemployment problem will help us create a complete picture of young people's situation within that age, which will help us understand youth unemployment from a more fundamental and comprehensive basis.

Youth unemployment rate is the figure that we most often read in newspapers or websites to show us the employment situation of young people. It does help us to get useful information about youth labor force and through the presentation of movement of this figure, we could get some basic insights about the situation that young people currently experience. However, it is not a perfect indicator to tell us what's happening in youth labor market, and thus could not help much when it comes to discuss the solutions of youth unemployment crisis. In fact, some more accurate measurements, such as youth unemployment ratio or NEET rate[i], have gained popularity in the analysis of youth unemployment problem, and I will discuss these two additional figures later on.

1.2 The latest youth unemployment crisis

It is widely recognized that the normal unemployment rate is higher than 0, and similarly, there has always been certain level of youth unemployment rate. At least in the late 1970s of America, there appeared researches targeting at youth unemployment problem. For example, Richard V.L. Cooper from the Rand Corporation published a

---

[i] NEET rate: The rate of youth not in employment, education and training

paper[11] titled *Youth Labor Market and the Military* in March 1978, in which he wrote the following words: "youth unemployment has become an increasingly important problem in recent years."

While there it is, youth unemployment problem, especially youth unemployment from a global perspective, has been hiding far away from the attention of the general public. This situation changes starting from 2008, when there was global financial crisis and a significant decline of economy, which intensified the tough employment situation that young people were experiencing. A large number of young people were scared for unemployment and got angry, and their anger burst out. Quickly, media noticed the occurring of youth unemployment crisis, and they spread this information to every corner of the world.

Descriptions like "Generation jobless" began to appear on the websites of many big media firms. In November 2011, The Wall Street Journal published an article titled *Generation Jobless: For Those Under 24, a Portrait in Crisis*[12], in which they stated that young people in America were experiencing "one of the toughest job markets" in modern history, and the youth actually suffered more than the old. They showed that up to the time the article was finished, unemployment rate of young adults had been higher than 16% for 32 months, and for a comparison purpose, the longest period that this figure stayed above 16% in the history was 23 months, and it happened during the downturn from 1982 to 1983.

In November 2012, Richard Blackden's article titled Youth Unemployment: *The Big Issue for the World's Economy*[13] appeared in the website of The Telegraph. In the article, Blackden related the words of Larry Summers, former Treasury Secretary of USA, and stated that youth unemployment problem was perhaps the most important long-term issue that America was facing. Later in April 2013, The Economist website published an article with a titled that was quite straightforward: *Generation Jobless*. This article provided a detailed and a relatively comprehensive exhibition of the world's youth unemployment crisis and it estimated that nearly 300 million young people globally didn't have a job. This situation, as was illustrated in the article, was even worse when took into consideration of those who didn't belong to labor force, such as those who had dropped out of labor force and got further worsened when included the effect of unpredicted movement of external environment.

The following two figures exhibit the movement of youth unemployment rates for the world from 2006 to 2014, with figure 1.1 showing the situation of three different regions and figure 1.2 exhibiting the situation of several countries that are independently selected.

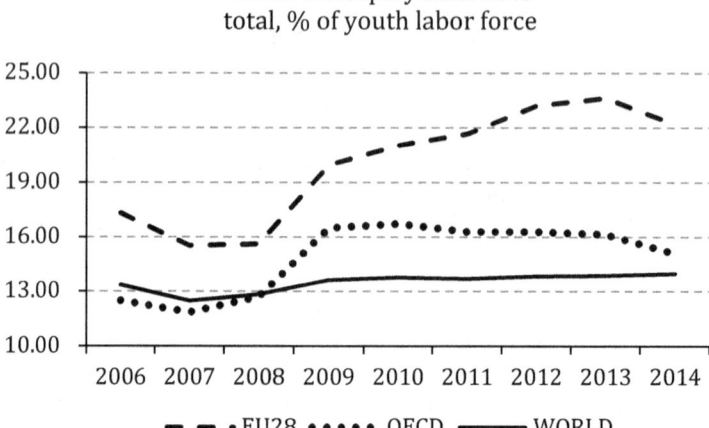

Figure 1.1 Youth unemployment rate for different regions

Source: OECD[14], World Bank[15]

From figure 1.1, we could see that for the world as a whole, youth unemployment rate rises slightly from 2007 to 2008, and has remained above 13% since 2008. The phenomenon of rising youth unemployment rates is more apparent for OECD countries and European Union countries.

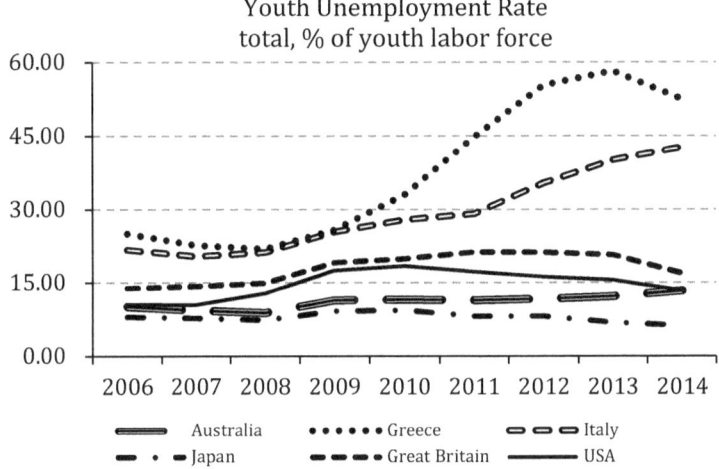

Figure 1.2 Youth unemployment rate for different countries

Source: OECD[16]

Figure 1.2 exhibits a similar pattern as figure 1.1, with the situation of Greece and Italy being much worse than the rest countries.

No wonder media would use "Generation Jobless" to describe youth unemployment crisis that the world is currently faced with: the absolute level of youth unemployment rate is really high, and the scale is on a global basis, which has influenced most countries, especially some developed ones. As a result, how to deal with youth unemployment crisis has become a pressing issue for the whole world.

1.3 The harm of youth unemployment for the public

The impact of youth unemployment crisis exists all around our society, which could be introduced from two aspects—on the youth themselves, and on the society. In this section, I will provide a brief explanation of the harm of youth unemployment crisis on the society and later, I will complete this illustration of the harm of youth unemployment crisis—from the perspective of the youth themselves. One thing needs to be mentioned that just like many other parts of this book, the discussions made here are largely based on the situation of Europe, and this is not only because data and relevant researches are mostly available for this region, but also because it is this region that youth unemployment problem, just as we have shown before, is most severe.

The cost of youth unemployment problem to the society could be summarized from two perspectives: one is from a short-term perspective and the other is from the long-term. From a short-term point of view, the most obvious cost is the fund needed to support those youth who have no sources of income due to unemployment. In October 2012, The Guardian published an article[17], sin which they introduce the content of a report made by Eurofund, and states that Europeans aged between 15 and 29 who belong to the group of people called NEETs have reached historical level high and are costing the EU €3 billion a week, a number which is a 28% increase since 2008. According to the same report, the total cost to EU members associated with the rising of number of NEETs is estimated to be €153 billion a year, nearly 1.2% of the region's GDP.

While NEETs doesn't equal to the group of unemployed youth, and losses caused by NEETs population and the unemployed youth are different, they are closely related to each other, and it does make sense to obtain a rough understanding about the short-term financial burden lead by youth unemployment crisis to the society based on that of the NEETs population. Besides, the cost to the society of youth unemployment crisis in the long-term is even more severe, which is not limited to the aspect of economy.

In the long-term, some of today's unemployed youth may still need public welfare support. Researches and studies have indicated that those who have experienced unemployment in their start-up period of career tend to have more problems concerning employment as they become older and have higher risk than other people to fall into long-term unemployment[18,19,20]. This is especially a problem when early day's unemployment lasts for long periods, in which case the society has to pay more for increased welfare expenditure.

Meantime, there are still concerns for the loss of production in the long run, which is probably more burdensome than the situation we are currently experiencing. Generally speaking, we human beings' skills will keep developing as we become older, and thus for a typical person, his unemployment at a younger age is supposed to cause less loss in production of the society compared with his unemployment at an older age, since as he becomes older, he is expected to possess higher level of skills which means higher level of importance and higher productivity. This partly explains why today's youth unemployment problem also matters so much for production in the future. Researchers have found that those who experience long-term unemployment at early age tend to have more problems to build high-level skills, and an estimation made by McKinsey Global Institute states that "by 2020 there will be a global shortfall of 85 million high- and middle-skilled workers."[21]

What's more, youth unemployment problem could incur cost to other aspects of human society. Up to now, my illustration mainly focuses on the economic part, but in reality, youth unemployment may also lay mines on the society—a potential risk of social problems, and this is mainly due to the fact that proper employment is important for a typical human being. As is shown in Professor McQuaid's summary[22], having a proper job will not only brings in wealth, so as to keep living standards above a certain level, but also plays a role like that of compass, which enables a person to have a proper direction in life. Without a job, especially for longer periods, young people will accumulate huge pressure, which may cause harm to their mental health as well as physical health. As the number of people in this situation increase dramatically in a society, there may gather up high risk of social unrest.

Youth unemployment crisis has cost our society much and may even cost more in the future. No wonder the following words once made by former US Treasury Secretary Larry Summers: "I'm not sure that there is a more important long-term issue than youth unemployment."[23]

1.4 One representative of current solutions: Youth Guarantee

To deal with current youth unemployment crisis, many governmental solutions have been carried out, and the Youth Guarantee project is perhaps the most ambitious and influential one. This Youth Guarantee project attempts to ensure that in EU, "all young people under the age of 25-year-old receive a good quality offer of employment, continued education, apprenticeship, or traineeship within a period of four months of becoming unemployed or leaving formal education".[24] To achieve this goal, €21 billion[25] is needed per year according to the estimation of ILO, and this project mainly covers three parts: to create more job trainings, more enterprises and the inclusion of the most vulnerable.

This Youth Guarantee project represents the key focus of current methods to handle youth unemployment: job creation. For example, in the G20 summit in Pittsburgh in September 2009, a strong mandate of "putting quality jobs at the heart of recovery" is reinforced and it includes "jobs creation, social protection, training, decent work and ILO fundamental principles and rights at work."[26] And in April 2010, a news titled *ILO Welcomes G-20 Labour and Employment Ministers' Recommendations on Job-Rich Recovery*[27] was published on the website of the ILO.

There are also suggestions based on limiting immigration, for fear that immigrants would grasp those job opportunities that are supposed to be taken up by local residents, and policies following the same methodology—to transfer jobs from foreigners to local youth, such as the efforts that the government of USA is currently taking: encouraging manufacturing companies to set up plants within the territory of the US.

In short, current solutions from governmental level mainly target at job creation and try to provide more jobs to those unemployed youth.

1.5 Characteristics and rationalities of current solutions

Current governmental solutions for youth unemployment focus on job creation, and there are common characteristics among these solutions.

Firstly, consider a weakened economy lead by the latest financial crisis as a key reason and accordingly, to create more job positions is of top priority. The 2008 financial crisis does have imposed a very harmful impact on Europe's economy, as well as the overall economic situation. Due to weakened economic conditions, production is cut and relatively fewer jobs are available for the large amount of youth who just step out of school with an urgent need of work.

Secondly, highlight differences among different countries in the understanding of youth unemployment crisis. Methods having been carried out recognize the particularities of situations in different countries and take those differences into the consideration of analysis of the causes as well as solutions of youth unemployment. For example, weak economy in Spain and Portugal have been used to explain their extremely high youth unemployment rates and labor law of France is often been considered as a factor that makes it more difficult for young people in France to get jobs. In each country's efforts of dealing with youth unemployment problem, proposed mechanisms typically vary based on different economic conditions, policy status and cultures.

Thirdly, target at those youth aged between 15 and 24. This is a key characteristic of current solutions, which may be more important than we have realized. The group of young people that could get help is limited to a specific age range—aged between 15 and 24, and this is consistent with the definition of youth unemployment. In other words, from the perspective of young people, they could get access to those help only when they are aged between 15 and 24, and if they are younger than 15 or older than 24, no such help will be available.

In short, concerning how to tackle youth unemployment problem, government's efforts are proposed mainly base on the acknowledgement that there are not enough jobs provided to the youth: when there are fewer jobs than the number of young people who seek employment, what government needs to do is to create more jobs. However, does the belief hold that unemployment rate rises for the economic decline (and thus fewer job opportunities) and to reduce youth unemployment rate we must create more jobs?

There are fundamental rationalities lying behind this belief, which could also be understood from three aspects: one is the current situation that many youths do not have jobs, the second is the timing that this youth unemployment crisis burst out following the 2008 financial crisis, and the last is the conventional logic between economic growth rate and unemployment rate.

Firstly, current situation creates a matter of urgency. Many researchers have been studying the adverse effect of unemployment at a young age, and there are at least two concerns among these studies. One focuses on the relationship between youth unemployment and stresses, and states that unemployment, especially long-period unemployment, tends to increase the level of stress people feel, which may finally harm physical health and mental health. The other examines the long-term effect of youth unemployment on people's career and figures out that those who have experienced unemployment in a young age tend to have larger possibility than others to experience unemployment in the future. As a result, those unemployed youth need jobs, need jobs right now, and otherwise their future might be compromised. Thus, to try to create more job positions is in any case a correct choice.

Secondly, the timing that youth unemployment crisis burst out following the 2008 financial crisis. During this period of panic, people first noticed the bankruptcy of some influential financial service groups, and then realized the coming of global financial crisis and later got astonished by the destructive power of this financial crisis. Only after this first round of panic, people noticed the rising of youth unemployment rate and realized the arriving of youth unemployment crisis. Youth unemployment crisis burst out right after financial crisis, and people's worry about it followed the panic of economic decline lead by financial crisis, and then, it is naturally to consider that youth unemployment crisis occurs as a result of economic decline, or the reduction of number of job positions. Once a reduced number of jobs are believed to trigger youth unemployment crisis, to create more jobs becomes a reasonable solution to lower down youth unemployment rate. In fact, there are researches recently stating that youth unemployment does drive mainly by economic decline, such as statement that "for younger individuals the difficulties are more related to the business cycle"[28].

Thirdly, the conventional logic between growth rate of economy and unemployment rate. There is a ready-made policy instrument, a solution to tackle unemployment problem that has been tested and verified by real-life experience. This solution follows the logic that when the economy is in the up channel, demand is high, and so is the number of job positions available for people. As the number of jobs increases, unemployment rate will go down. In turn, during economic decline, demand is weak and so is economic activity. The number of job openings thus declines and when fewer jobs are available, it will become harder for people to find employment and unemployment rate will then rise.

This logic is often illustrated using the Philips Curve, a line roughly exhibiting the adverse relationship between unemployment rate and inflation rate. Since inflation rate is typically a signal of economic status—when the economy expands, inflation rate tends to rise and when the economy declines, inflation rate tends to fall, and thus the Phillips Curve could be considered as one line revealing the adverse relationship between the level of economic activity and unemployment rate. Short-term Phillips Curve has been used to guide policy makers: when unemployment rate is too high, government will usually boost up economy to stimulate supply as well as demand, so as to create large amount of job positions and finally lower down unemployment rate. If we consider youth unemployment as one part of unemployment, it is natural to try to create more jobs when faced with rising youth unemployment rate.

To conclude, solutions that have been carried out to tackle youth unemployment problem—with the focus of creating more jobs and trainings, are reasonable and have a solid foundation.

2. TO EXPLORE MORE ABOUT YOUTH UNEMPLOYMENT

2.1 Outcome and worries of current solutions

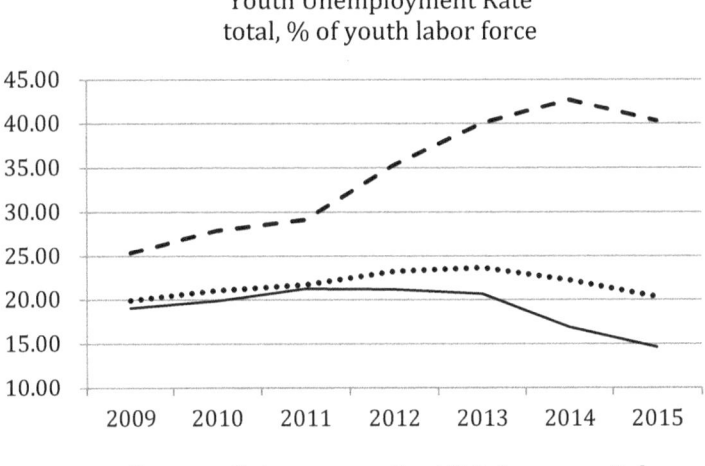

Figure 2.1 Youth unemployment rate for selected regions in Europe

Source: OECD[29]

Figure 2.1 exhibits the movement of youth unemployment rates from 2009 to 2015 of three selected regions: European Union, Great Britain and Italy. European Union is the place where the Youth Guarantee project is implemented, the Great Britain is a typical developed country that has been suffering from youth unemployment crisis this time, and Italy is one of those countries that get hit most by youth unemployment crisis. As is showing in the figure, youth unemployment rate for

European peaked in 2013, and then fell down gradually. For Great Britain, this trend started two years earlier, in which case the figure fell slightly in 2012 and 2013, and then fell significantly in 2014. And even for Italy, youth unemployment rate started to fall in 2014. The changes of youth unemployment rate show us an optimistic and encouraging result of efforts that have been implemented.

Figure 2.1 provides a visual exhibition of the results of current efforts—falling of youth unemployment rate from both a country-specific perspective and a European Union perspective, which is indeed encouraging. However, alongside with these achievements, disturbing messages arising from different stakeholders of current arrangements.

On one hand, it seems that training programs provided are not so attractive for young people, who are supposed to benefit directly from these trainings. An article titled *Almost One in Four Apprentices Drop Out*[30] reveals some worrisome phenomenon in England. This article related figures from the Department for Business, Innovation and Skills (BIS)[i] of UK and showed that around 23.6% apprentices gave up apprenticeship program from 2010 to 2011, just a slight improvement compared with one year before. And by comparing with this figure from 2009 to 2010, which was 7.2%, this article concluded that "Apprenticeship system is having more difficulty trying to retain students."

This article didn't tell us why such a high percent of participants preferred to quit apprenticeship program, even though the UK government has agreed "to encourage more employers to offer the on-the-job training scheme and sees apprenticeships as a real alternative to university."[31] Perhaps, young people quit because while there have set up many projects to put them into jobs or trainings, these actions are in such a hurry that the organizers do not take the ambition and willingness of those youth into consideration. Time is so limited that people cannot hesitate to think about whether those job positions provided to the youth match their interests and capacities. If positions provided are not the kind of jobs that the youth want, it is possible that they are unwilling to do what they are expected to do and thus the attractiveness of those training programs, as well as the effectiveness, are weakened.

Not alone students, but also employers exhibit kind of suspicious

---

[i] This department has merged with another department and is called Department for Business, Energy and Industrial Strategy (BEIS)

attitude about apprenticeship mechanism. In February 2012, The Telegraph published an article titled *Employers Warn on 'quickie apprenticeships'*[32], in which the author related words of a HR manager from one housing group and stated that quickie apprenticeships as many companies offered might not be the kind of apprenticeships that youth people desired. And another article[33] showed that in the beginning of 2012, the IT department of an involved company had decided to postpone its apprentices to review the content of their programs.

Different from young people, employers' doubts are based on more concrete considerations. On one hand, they worry that current apprenticeship mechanisms only last for relatively short period of time, which may be too short to guarantee a proper employment for the youth when these training programs end. For example, The Telegraph related a report issued by National Audit Office (NAO), in which there were data showing that from 2010 to 2011, 3% apprenticeships lasted for less than 12 weeks and 19% were less than 6 months[34]. And data from the same report disclosed that for the reason of training arrangements being too short, around 90 training providers were under investigation. Besides duration issues, employers are also concerned with the quality of contents of the apprenticeship programs. Again, in the article *Employers Warn on 'quickie apprenticeships'*, the author related words from the Chartered Institute of Personnel and Development of UK, who encouraged apprenticeships "focus on improving quality"; and words from a skills advisor, Katerina Rüdiger, mentioned that young people should be at the center of apprenticeships, who were expected to become professionals through these apprenticeships.

As a result, even though in the short-term, youth unemployment rate may fall due to a quick supply of apprenticeship programs, those unemployed youth may not be able to benefit much from these arrangements, since these arrangements would less likely guarantee a proper employment in the future. And this means a sudden increase in supply of job positions may not be as helpful as we hope from a long-term perspective.

What makes this situation even more worrisome is the fact that due to cost issues, these apprenticeship programs may not be able to last long, which, in other words, they may not be sustainable but just exist as a temporary aid. In June, 2014, This Is Money website published an article titled *Small Firms Warn Funding Cuts May Stop the Boom in Apprentice Jobs in Its Tracks and Hit Young Workers*[35], which stated that in the Great Britain, fully funded apprenticeships would cease by August, 2015, and employers "will need to pay up to a third of future apprenticeship training costs, as well as designing and running courses with colleges", and then, apprenticeship positions might decline significantly. The article related research from the Electrical Contractors Association that as high as 94% businesses would reduce or simply ceased apprenticeship positions for the extra burden. Employers have their own worries, such as young people might leave their firms after getting trained, which would make these firms receiving nothing for bearing the cost as well as risk of providing training programs.

A conclusion of discussions above is that while apprenticeship mechanisms have gained great confidence and youth unemployment rate does fall compared with that of years before, to which extent would those unemployed youth benefit from these mechanisms still remain unclear, since just as many employers have been concerned with, some apprenticeship programs last just too short a period and their contents may not be able to help young people build their own competencies. Thus, if we look beyond the need to lower down youth unemployment rate right now and examine the long-term effects of our methods to help today's unemployed youth, we may not be as optimistic as we have been.

In short-term, a sudden boost of job supply will significantly lower down youth unemployment rate and thus comfort the social concern about the employment situation that young people experience, but to which extent those youth could benefit from these quick-provided jobs, interns or trainings remind unclear. This is a key insight that promotes us to move further and think more about solutions of youth unemployment problem: while youth unemployment rates have fallen, we are still puzzled and curious about desired solutions.

2.2 Puzzles about the reason of youth unemployment

While short-term results of apprenticeship mechanisms are encouraging, there exist worries and some defects have emerged. Currently, there is relatively less knowledge concerning youth unemployment and when youth unemployment problem is treated as the generalized unemployment issue, it is reasonable to try to boost economy and provide more job positions. Even if there is significant difference between youth unemployment and the general unemployment, the effort of providing more jobs could also be justified, since those unemployed youth, in any case, need it.

However, if we move a step further, and set aside the consideration of current situation of youth unemployment problem, and then rather than discussing how to help today's unemployed youth, we would come across a new question—how to prevent youth unemployment problem from recurring in the future? Relatively few researches have tried hard enough to explore the causes of youth unemployment problem, since the cause—at least as it looks like, is much apparent, which is there doesn't exist enough job positions available for young people due to a weakened macroeconomic condition.

To create more jobs is considered as the top priority in methods that have been carried out to tackle youth unemployment problem, but there is little clarification and explanation about whether we are targeting at tackling youth unemployment problem or we are focusing on the current needs of those unemployed youth. A possible illustration is that our focus of creating more jobs is to fulfill the needs of current unemployed youth, but not for dealing with youth unemployment problem, and if the general public take the intent of our creating more jobs as tacking youth unemployment problem, they may form a wrong understanding of the causes of youth unemployment problem.

In face of youth unemployment issue, we need to distinguish between two things: one is the current situation that large amount of youths does not have jobs and the other is the subject of youth unemployment problem. These two things are actually different from each other, and if we only focus on the first one, which is to ease current stressful situation, all we need to do is to put those young people into trainings or job positions. However, if we want to deal with the second one, that pay attention to youth unemployment problem and prevent it from recurring in the future, we have to think a lot more about our efforts. If we mix the current situation due to youth unemployment problem with the topic of youth unemployment problem itself, we may not be able to design our mechanism base on the right target, and this is likely the reason that why current methods of creating more jobs or trainings have aroused arguments and worries from different stakeholders.
It is true that current actions to create more jobs are helpful and is of great necessity, but do we believe that to lower down youth unemployment rate is equal to conquer youth unemployment problem? To which extend youth unemployment rate represents youth unemployment problem and if the result of youth unemployment problem is an increased youth unemployment rate, what is the cause of youth unemployment problem? Or rather, does youth unemployment problem equal to an increased youth unemployment rate? If we consider youth unemployment problem and the rising of youth unemployment rate as the same thing, we inherently hold that the causes and results of youth unemployment problem exist simultaneously: young people having no jobs (fewer labor demand than labor supply) is

To explore more about youth unemployment

not only the result of youth unemployment problem, but also its cause. But is it true that the cause and result of youth unemployment problem exist simultaneously?

There is a possibility that it is not true. And consider a question like this: is it possible that those youth's failure in finding jobs is due to factors exist long before they enter job market? This is a reasonable question since things happened in the past could have an impact over things in the future and there is a possibility—just for the purpose of getting a full picture of youth unemployment problem—that things occurred in the past have indicated youth's failure of finding jobs. If so, we must target on things in the past to propose solutions, otherwise our efforts won't be as effective as we hope.

Let's use an example to understand the rationality of this approach: A factory keeps pulling wasted water into the river, which causes harm to the fish in the river and thus affects the benefits of people living on the fish in the downstream. This simplified example has nothing to do with young people's unemployment and here in my book, I use it to illustrate one kind of logic, which may also be applied to the analysis of youth unemployment.

Picture 2.1 shows the river, and point A locates in the upstream while point C locates in the downstream. Water arises from the mountain, passes through A then C and finally flows into the lake. One day, a printing factory is set up close to point B, a place near A, and this factory keeps pouring wasted water into the river. Very soon, water in the river starting from point B is polluted. Now, people who live on fish in the lake have troubles, since more and more fish in the lake die due to toxic substance carried by the polluted water. To protect fish in the lake, people decide to purify the water of the river before it flows into the lake. For this purpose, they set up a purification facility near the estuary of the river, at point D, and water will be purified before pouring into the lake. Shortly after this arrangement, residents are released and are delighted to fish again.

To explore more about youth unemployment

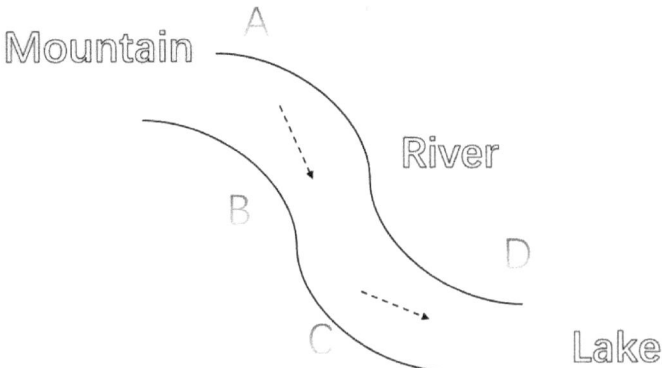

Picture 2.1 The example of a river

However, this pleasure doesn't last long, since shortly after the purification facility beginning its operation, residents there find the cost to operate this facility is so high that they cannot afford to use it for long. However, polluted water keeps coming and people get worried again. Suppose residents living in location C send a team of representatives walking backward along the river, trying to find the source of pollution. They find the printing factory and negotiate with the owner of that factory, coming up with a plan to establish a purifying facility in the production line of the factory so that wasted water will be purified first before flowing into the river. While the operation of the purifying facility still costs a lot, it would be certainly lower than the original method which aims to purify water at the estuary of the river. And once for all, residents do not need to worry for polluted water and enjoy their fish finally.

The same rationality could be applied to our understanding of youth unemployment problem. For the river, water is observed to be polluted at point D yet the printing factory locates at point B, and for the unemployed youth, does the reason that they fail to get a job exists at the time they leave school to find employment, or much earlier before they try to seek employment—as point B (rather than D) in the example of the river? We notice that young people cannot find jobs when they enter job market, but we have to ask: does the reason of this phenomenon lie in the time they enter job market, or much earlier before they enter job market?

Current discussions and proposed solutions of youth unemployment problem mainly come from a macro point of view, which focuses on macro factors such as economic environment to understand the causes of youth unemployment problem. And accordingly, more job positions are needed. Solutions proposed like this are of great value, since they could provide young people jobs right away and possibly prevent them from falling into long-term unemployment due to a lack of work experience. But there are also concerns that these mechanisms may not be the ultimate solutions and may not benefit the youth from a long-term point of view (as is discussed in section 2.1). Besides the concern for lack of job positions, there is also a preference to analyze youth unemployment problem based on various demographic factors of different regions.

While I recognize the rationality behind these approaches, I am wondering that is there a more generalized way to analyze youth unemployment problem? Or rather, is there a universal way that we could analyze the causes of youth unemployment and thus actions needed to conquer youth unemployment regardless of specific conditions in each country?

A piece of news published on website The Telegraph may give us an insight about this idea. The article was titled *Arnold Clark: More Than 80% of Apprentice Applicants 'unemployable'*[36], and was published on 22 May 2012. As was written in the news, one monitoring group found that among its 2,280 youngsters who applied for apprenticeships in the company, 1,850 (or 81%) were simple "unemployable". According to this group, many applicants do not have a proper attitude or required communication skills, and do not possess a basic knowledge of standards expected except for unrealistic illusions about themselves. And this phenomenon becomes worse due to "their 'inability to make a decision based on anything other than 'I want!'" and "a 'zero understanding' of the negative consequences of their actions". According to the article, there are some youth who do not know how to perform properly in work environment.

In fact, youth unemployment problem is more complex than we have realized now, and to fully understand the nature and the whole picture of youth unemployment problem, there is a need to look beyond current situation to examine more facts, facts exist before the time that the youth entering job market and facts beyond what we have noticed up to now—while current efforts to create more jobs are essential, they are not sustainable, especially from a long-term point of view. We still need to explore more about the causes of youth unemployment problem, which may help us ease youth unemployment problem forever in the future.

2.3 Historical youth unemployment rate

One constructive way to explore more about youth unemployment problem is to have a look at the path of historical movement of youth unemployment rate. Due to data availability, I will only demonstrate figure of the whole world starting from late 1990s and figures of United States as well as Japan since 1950s.

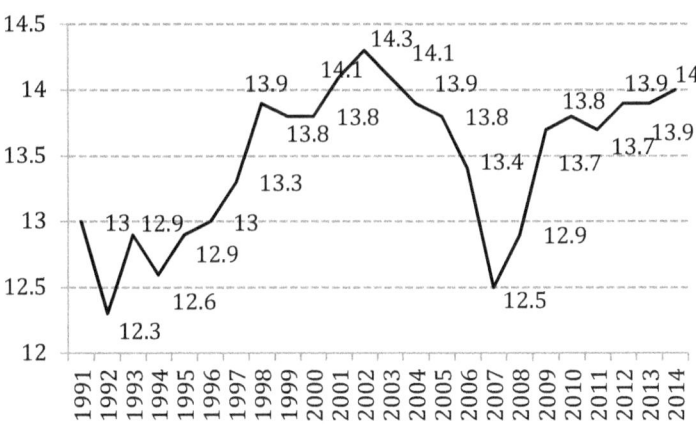

Figure 2.2 Youth unemployment rate of the world

Source: World Bank; ILO, Key Indicators of the Labour Market database.

Figure 2.2 exhibits historical youth unemployment rates for the world, and there exist a peak and a bottom. One key insight is that throughout the years, there is always certain level of youth unemployment. Just as the fact that there is "natural rate of unemployment"[i], or "long-run

---

[i] Nature rate of unemployment or the following long-run equilibrium unemployment rate, is typically composed of frictional unemployment and structural unemployment, and does not equal to zero because no matter in which condition, there will always be some people looking for jobs

equilibrium unemployment rate", for youth unemployment rate, when it stays below certain level, it would be considered as "natural" and "acceptable", in which case there is no need to worry about youth unemployment. And this is why there always exists certain level of youth unemployment rate, yet the general public only notice and care about it when the rate rises significantly following the year of 2008.

Let's pay attention to the situation from 1998 to 2006[i], during which period worldwide youth unemployment rate stayed above 13.8% and peaked in 2002, which was 14.3%. Until now, it remains as an unanswered question in this book that whether it is macro-economic factors that lead to youth unemployment crisis, even though it is no doubt that macro-economic factors such as the level of economic prosperity will affect unemployment rate, and youth unemployment rate, to a certain degree.

Under the hypothesis that macro-economic factors determine the occurring of youth unemployment crisis, when economic conditions worsen, youth unemployment rate will rise. Let's use data of the globe to check whether this negative relationship exists between these two variables.

---

[i] Youth unemployment rate for 1998 and 2006 were 13.9% and 13.4% respectively

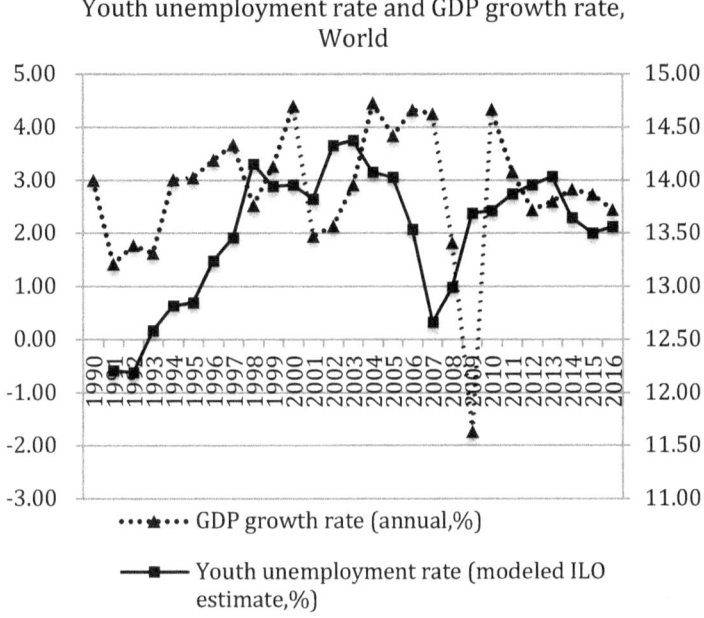

Figure 2.3 youth unemployment rate and GDP growth rate of the world

Source: World Bank[37,38]

Figure 2.3 exhibits the paths of youth unemployment rate and GDP growth rate, from which we could get an intuitive idea about the role of macro-economic factors in the occurring of youth unemployment crisis. Remember that when youth unemployment rate isn't too high, it doesn't constitute a problem and it remains acceptable until it reaches above certain level, and here, let's suppose youth unemployment crisis turns up when youth unemployment rate rises above 13.5%[i]. Now we find two periods of youth unemployment crisis from figure 2.3, with the first one starting at 1997, ending at 2006, and the second one lasting from 2009 to 2015.

As we can see from the figure, at the beginning of these two periods,

---

[i] I choose the number of 13.5% just for the purpose of analysis here, which hasn't been endorsed by academic researches

the rate of GDP growth both declined, which dropped from 3.67% to 2.52% from 1997 to 1998 and dropped from 1.82% to -1.74% from 2008 to 2009. And this does indicate that economic condition probably determines the occurring of youth unemployment crisis. What's more, at the end of these two periods, GDP growth rate had both risen, as is shown from 2005 to 2006, and from 2014 to 2015.

While there is pattern like this, we cannot conclude that economic condition dominates the existing of youth unemployment crisis, since movements of youth unemployment rate and GDP growth rate do not match with each other perfectly enough. For example, from 2001 to 2003, as well as from 2014 to 2015, the two of them moved in the same direction. And if we take the period from 1993 to 1997 into consideration, we would find these two figures have moved in the same direction for consecutive 4 years.

As a result, we could not state that the declining of macroeconomic conditions would certainly lead to youth unemployment crisis, since apparently, the occurring of youth unemployment crisis is not only affected by macroeconomic conditions. This means we should not emphasize too much on macroeconomic conditions when dealing with youth unemployment problem.

Besides macroeconomic factors, country-specific factors may also play a key role in the formation of youth unemployment crisis. An intuitive way is to have a look at historical youth unemployment rates for different countries.

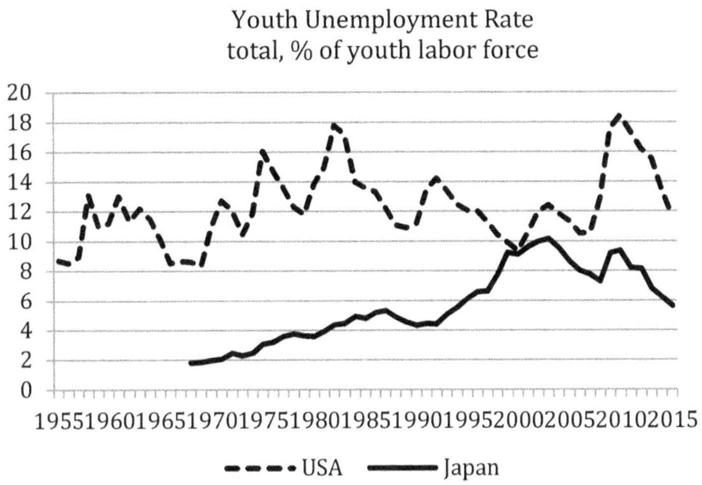

Youth Unemployment Rate
total, % of youth labor force

Figure 2.4 Youth unemployment rate for the USA and Japan

Source: OECD[39]

Figure 2.4 exhibits historical youth unemployment rates for the USA and Japan respectively, and they are indeed different from each other. We could find that before 21th century, the paths of youth unemployment rates are significantly different between United States and Japan, since for US, youth unemployment rate fluctuated at a relatively high level, around 12%, while for Japan, the rate rose gradually from late 1960s to the middle of 1980s and rose once again until early 2000s. When it comes to the 21th century, even though the general trend of movement of youth unemployment rates is largely the same between these two countries, the absolute level of these two figures is not the same.

In fact, youth unemployment rates of many countries did rise significantly after 2008, but there are also countries whose youth unemployment rates have been rising steadily before 2008: France, United Kingdom, Hungary, Sweden and Mexico have such a pattern of youth unemployment rate. There are even countries whose youth unemployment rates have been declining, even during the period of this latest financial crisis. Luxembourg could be categorized in this group, although its youth unemployment rate has shown a rising trend before 2008. Germany is a more obvious case, with youth unemployment rate peaked in 2005, and falls gradually since then. There are countries whose youth unemployment rates have reached at historical level high, such as Poland and Slovak Republic, and there are also countries whose youth unemployment rates have been declining, such as Chile and Israel.[40]

An apparent conclusion of this section is that macroeconomic factors do play a crucial role in explaining the occurring of youth unemployment crisis, and so do country's specific factors. Noticing that the method of using GDP growth rate to act as a proxy variable of macroeconomic conditions may not be sound, and to use the data of the world as a basis for analysis may not be able to reveal an accurate relationship between youth unemployment rate and GDP growth rate, since there are too many factors included in world's GDP as well as youth unemployment rate, and some of these factors may play a role contradicting that of another. But just as readers will find in the later part of this book, the conclusion of this section will not affect the conclusion of this book: whether macroeconomic factors being important or not, analysis of youth unemployment problem from the perspective of labor-supply is of great necessity.

2.4 Financial crisis and youth unemployment crisis

Based on discussion in the former section, we have found the rationality behind the statement that youth unemployment problem is driven by macroeconomic factors and influenced by country-specific factors, but our exploration will not end up here, since there is an obvious drawback of the judgment that we have just made—this finding and conclusion is of little help from a long-term perspective.

To understand this, let's have a look at two questions.

Question 1: would youth unemployment crisis recur in the future?

Answer: Highly likely.

The conclusion of financial crisis leading to youth unemployment crisis follows the logic that financial crisis reduces the demand for labor, and then, young people could not find jobs for a lack of job opportunities. Once demand of young labor weakens, youth unemployment rate rises, and when this figure reaches above a certain level, youth unemployment crisis recurs.

Question 2: when will youth unemployment crisis recurs?

Answer: Having no idea.

Identifying macroeconomic factors as the causes of youth unemployment crisis couldn't help us predict the timing of youth unemployment crisis, since we don't know when will macroeconomic factors worsen and a decline of labor demand could be triggered by many other factors, such as technical advancement, industrial transfer and natural disasters etc. As a result, our current knowledge, which highlights macroeconomic conditions such as financial crisis as the leading reason behind youth unemployment problem, contributes little in predicting the happening of youth unemployment crisis in the future, and if so, we could hardly state that we have fully identify and understand the reasons behind youth unemployment problem. Many different factors could affect labor demand, and thus the accuracy of predicting the occurring of youth unemployment crisis under current knowledge framework is limited.

When trying to understand the causes of youth unemployment problem, this book pays a special attention to the frequency of occurring of youth unemployment crisis (and the fluctuations of youth unemployment rate). This helps because when we understand this sort of things, we could possibly predict the recurring of youth unemployment crisis in the future and then to take actions now to prevent that from happening. Drawback of the statement that macroeconomic factors lead to youth unemployment crisis is that this conclusion has little value in prediction, and thus couldn't help us prevent youth unemployment crisis from recurring.

Until now, the question that suggested by the headline of this section remains unanswered, and now we will ask, what's the role of the 2008 financial crisis in the occurring of youth unemployment crisis this time?

To facilitate this analysis, let's introduce two statements:

1) In the past 50 years, there exists young people's unemployment, but for much of the period youth unemployment rate remained relatively low and thus has been hidden away from public's attention.

2) When there are some youths who cannot find jobs, it is not a problem, and only when too many youths cannot find jobs, in which case youth unemployment rate rises above certain level, it becomes a

problem.

Once we reach consensus about the two statements made above, we understand that the role of macroeconomic factors (specifically, this 2008 financial crisis) is to make youth unemployment situation, which always exists, more severe. A role sounds similar? Yes, its function is just like that of catalyst in a chemical reaction process.

The role of catalyst in a chemical reaction process is to accelerate the reaction process, which would make a slow, unapparent reaction become fast and prominent. This is exactly the role of financial crisis in the occurring of youth unemployment crisis. Before the bursting out of this latest financial crisis, there exists certain level of youth unemployment, and this situation stays far away from attention of the general public. Financial crisis drags down the growth rate of economy, which reduces the demand for labor and thus worsens the situation of young job seekers. This has made their finding employment more difficult and finally drives up youth unemployment rate, globally. As we all know, whether a chemical reaction process will happen or not depends not on catalyst, the character of which remains unchanged during the reaction process, but on the nature of the two or more chemicals that are involved directly in the chemical reaction. And when it comes to discuss the causes of youth unemployment problem, if macroeconomic factors play a role like that of catalyst, we cannot help asking, what's the nature or fundamental characteristics of youth unemployment problem then?

In fact, if we consider youth unemployment as a problem only when it becomes severe, which means there is no youth unemployment problem during periods when youth unemployment rate remains relatively low, and then we could confidently state that the 2008 financial crisis is the key reason of youth unemployment crisis this time. But there is a drawback for this judgment, since it could not help us prevent youth unemployment problem from recurring in the future. For example, we don't know when will financial crisis burst out again, and thus we don't know when we should take actions to deal with the occurring of youth unemployment crisis. What's worse, not only financial crisis, but also other events could drive up youth unemployment rates, such as advancement of technology or trade war between countries.

The bursting out of financial crisis doesn't necessarily have a real impact on the employment prospect and career path of a particular person—this is a statement that is relatively reasonable when we realize that having no jobs for specific periods of time may not necessarily indicate a poor career status: for example, many students prefer a gap year to travel before graduation and seeking employment. We care about youth unemployment problem because it relates to young people's employment status in the future, and if the employment prospect of young people doesn't get affected, we won't worry about their unemployment. And thus, we could not state that macroeconomic factors explain the whole story of youth unemployment problem.

To conclude, while financial crisis drives up youth unemployment rate and leads to youth unemployment crisis, it cannot be considered as the only reason underlying youth unemployment problem for its lack of instructive significance in the future, especially concerning the recurring and frequency of youth unemployment crisis. When more factors relating to youth unemployment problem get better, it is possible that there wouldn't be youth unemployment crisis even if financial crisis bursts out, just as catalyst wouldn't make a chemical reaction happen if chemicals involved could not produce a chemical reaction. This encourages us to explore further about the reasons of youth unemployment problem.

2.5 Shortcomings of "Youth Unemployment Rate"

Youth unemployment rate is so high that it overwhelms our minds and since it is such a common phenomenon all over the world, media has used words such as "generation jobless" or "a lost generation" to describe the employment status of today's young people. While it is certain that the rate of youth unemployment does help us get some insight about youth unemployment problem, it is not as comprehensive as we have expected and thus this figure we often see in media and researches may not serve as an effective indicator. When we form a perception about youth unemployment problem through youth unemployment rate, we may get mislead, since youth unemployment rate may be a biased measure of the situation that young people are currently experiencing.

Youth unemployment rate is the percentage of the unemployed compared to the total labor force (both employed and unemployed) of that age group.

Thus,

$$Youth\ Unemployment\ Rate = \frac{Unemployed\ Youth_{15-24}}{Youth\ Labor\ Force_{15-24}}$$

To explore more about youth unemployment

When gathering data about unemployed people, total population is typically classified into three groups: employed, unemployed and economically inability (in other words, not included in the labor force). This methodology is also applied to the process of calculating youth unemployment rate. Based on ILO standards, young people (aged between 15 and 24) who study in school are excluded from calculation of labor force and they are considered as not in the labor market.

Then we have an equation here:

$$Youth\ Labor\ Force_{15-24} = Total\ Youth_{15-24} - Youth\ in\ Education_{15-24}$$

And the calculation that produces the figure we often see in media and researches is actually:

$$Youth\ Unemployment\ Rate = \frac{Unemployed\ Youth_{15-24}}{Total\ Youth_{15-24} - Youth\ in\ Education_{15-24}}$$

Since youth unemployment rate is equal to the number of unemployed youth divided by the number of youth labor force, when those young people who study at school are excluded from the calculation of labor force, the denominator of the formula is reduced—which results in an overstated youth unemployment measurement. When we add back those youth who have been classified as not belong to labor force (largely composed of those who study at school), the rate of youth unemployment falls instantly.

Eurostat introduces an alternative figure to indicate the situation of youth unemployment, which is named as Youth Unemployment Ratio. When calculating this ratio, Eurostat uses the total population (aged between 15 to 24) instead of just those in the labor force as the denominator:

$$Youth\ Unemployemnt\ Ratio = \frac{Unemployed\ Youth_{15-24}}{Total\ Youth_{15-24}}$$

Adjusted in this way, young people's employment situation presented by statistical data is significantly different, since "the youth unemployment ratio is by definition always smaller than the youth unemployment rate, typically less than half of it."[41] If we divide youth unemployment rate for euro zone in August 2013 by 2, it arrives at a level slightly higher than 6%, which seems not that worrisome.

This is the sort of fallacy that contained in the calculation of youth unemployment rate and now we get to know that the actual situation of young people's unemployment may not be as severe as we have thought of and the commonly used youth unemployment measurement actually overstates the employment status of young people. However, overstating the actual situation doesn't constitute a real problem compared with the possibility that our efforts carried out aiming to help the unemployed youth may miss the point, especially from a long-term point of view.

We cannot take it for granted that all the youth need help and take hasty actions before a clear understanding about what actually happens in job market and which group of youth need our help. Youth unemployment rate does not help much on this aspect, since by examining the calculation of youth unemployment rate we know that it exaggerates the actual situation.

Not every young person needs help and our support efforts may fall into a waste of time and resources if we do not target at the right group of people. For example, the calculation of youth unemployment rate only includes those youth who are out of school at the age between 15 and 24, and thus the proposed solution by revising education system to better prepare young people for employment may lead to a different result compared with our original purpose. This is because those youth who are not in tertiary education, especially those who could not get access to tertiary education due to cost or other problems, would not benefit from our methods of transforming education, simply because they are out of school. In this sense, to revise education system should also make it more affordable and accessible, and this is perhaps more important than revising the contents of education for the purpose of employment.

To conclude, facts revealed by youth unemployment rate are limited, which may also be misleading, and thus it is inappropriate for us to propose solutions without a careful examination of more information. Many researchers have begun to use long-term youth unemployment rate and labor participation ratio to help build a comprehensive view of youth unemployment issue, and this helps, especially from a long-term point of view with the purpose of preventing youth unemployment crisis from recurring.

2.6 To warm-up: new question arises as more facts being examined

In the former section, I state that the calculation of youth unemployment rate excludes those who are studying at school and point out that the phenomenon of rising youth unemployment rate mainly indicates the worrisome situation of those youths who are out of school, and thus our efforts of revising educational system to better prepare young people for employment may not contribute to the conquer of youth unemployment problem as we have expected. This insight helps but only partially, since at an age between 15 and 24, many young people might have already finished their high school study or college study, yet still have no jobs. Only for those study at school, the revising of educational materials helps.

Among those who enter job market at an age between 15 and 24, what's the percentage that has completed high school study? And for those who have completed high school, how many of them have went on pursuing a tertiary education? These questions could help us to estimate how much we should emphasize on revising education system just for employment purpose, and what measures should be taken. After all, the purposes, characteristics and teaching methods of different levels of education periods are different.

While education issue is important, there exists too much uncertainties and this book won't go further along this direction—education-related issues are not the focus of this book. Instead, let's consider a more concrete fact: the older typically have finished higher level of education than the younger. This may not be the case for specific individuals since one could finish their certain level of education at a younger age or older, but for a random sample of total population, this judgment is largely true. For example, when we encounter two strangers in a park, the possibility that the older has finished higher level of education than the younger is larger than the possibility that the younger has finished higher level of education. And this conclusion is especially true when we divide the age group of 15 to 24 into two parts: those aged between 15 and 19 and those aged between 20 and 24. When the difference in age comes at a range of 5 years (20-15, or 24-19), it is reasonable to state that among the total youths who enter job market at an age of 15-24, the older (aged between 20 and 24) generally have received higher education than the younger (aged between 15 and 19).

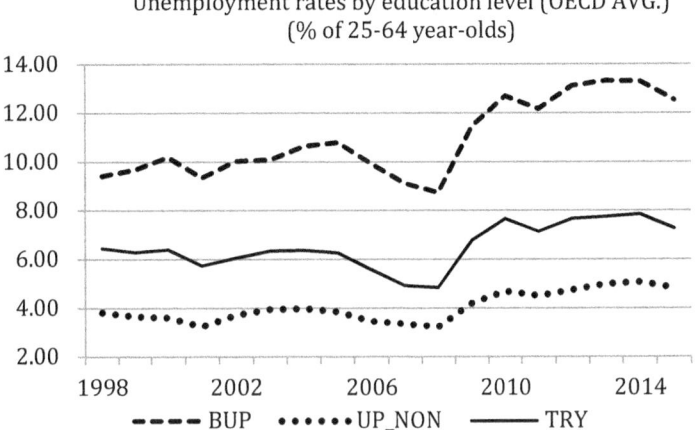

Figure 2.5 OECD's Unemployment rates by education level

Source: OECD[42]

Figure 2.5 exhibits unemployment rates by education level of OECD countries on average[i]. From this figure we could find that those have only completed below-upper secondary education have the highest unemployment rate, which is above 8% even at its lowest point, while for the other two educational cases, youth unemployment rate remains below 8% even for the highest point.

---

[i] Based on the introduction on the webpage of OECD, this figure shows "the unemployment rates of people according to their education levels: below upper secondary, upper secondary non-tertiary, or tertiary" by "measuring the percentage of unemployed 25-64 year-olds among 25-64 year-olds in the labor force."

To explore more about youth unemployment

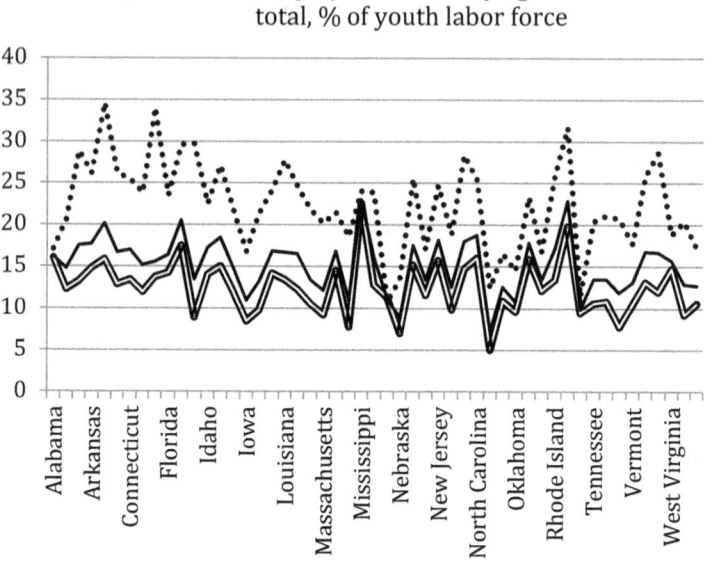

Figure 2.6 America's youth unemployment rates by age

Source: Governing[43], U.S. Bureau of Labor Statistics

Figure 2.6 exhibits the difference of unemployment rates among different age groups based on the data of the USA, from which we could find that employment situation of the younger group is much worse than that of the older, a phenomenon almost prevails in all states and in certain state such as California, youth unemployment rate of those aged of 16-19 is more than twice as that of those aged of 20-24.

A combination of findings of figure 2.5 and figure 2.6 actually support more or less the conclusion that the older typically have finished higher level of education than the younger. We know that those who only have a below-upper secondary education experience tend to suffer more from unemployment, and among the unemployed youth the younger group has a much higher unemployment rate. And, for those who enter job market at an age between 16 and 19[i], we could hardly expect that they have finished tertiary education. Suppose the number of labor force aged of 16-19 equals to that of those aged of 20-24, we could deduce that even for youth unemployment crisis this time, the crisis is more likely the crisis of the younger group, and if so, the methods of revising educational contents especially tertiary education won't help much, since those who need more help do not receive tertiary education.

Once we find the importance of tertiary education for young people's employment, the next question is to ask why many youths cannot get access to higher level of education or drop out of school during their study?

In a report titled as *Dropping Out of High School: Prevalence, Risk Factors and Remediation Strategies*[44], it is stated that factors associated with dropping out of high school include the following ones: low-income family background, less expectation from adults for them to perform well at school and less involvement of parents in their education. In another research, *Finishing High School: Alternative Pathways and Dropout Recovery*[45], Tyler and Lofstrom (2009) relate findings by Bridgeland et al. and states that "Students' family background greatly affects their educational outcomes and is commonly viewed as the most important predictor of schooling achievement." And in *Early School Leaving in Europe—Questions and Answers*[46], when asked why young people abandon education early, it replied, "Although the situation varies in different countries, early school leaving in Europe is strongly linked to social disadvantage and low education backgrounds."

Whether these researches trustworthy or not, one subject comes into our sight when discuss youth unemployment problem—family. Should family be included in the analysis of youth unemployment problem?

Up to now, my focus is to lead readers to think more about youth unemployment, with a key focus on looking beyond youth unemployment rate and review more fundamental facts. However, when we begin to examine more facts relating to youth unemployment problem, we come across contradictory feelings. On one hand, we feel released since the actual situation may not be as worse as is revealed by youth unemployment rate, since this rate isn't a perfect measure and tends to overstate the actual situation. On the other hand, we feel worried since our current methods carried out to conquer youth unemployment problem may not be effective enough and the

---

[i] Here I use 16-19 as the first part just in response to the data in chart 2-6, with 16-year-old being larger than the start point of calculation of youth unemployment rate: 15-year-old

employment prospect of those who have jobs may be worse than what we have expected—for example, Malik, S.(2012)[47] introduced a report made by the Eurofound, and stated that the number of employed young adults for 26 member states (of European Union) is at a historical low point, and "were working fewer hours and in less secure jobs". And "In 2011, 42% of young working Europeans were in temporary employment, up from just over a third a decade ago. A total of 30%, or 5.8 million young adults, were in part-time employment—an increase since 2001 of nearly nine percentage points."

All these stuffs mean, we need to explore more about youth unemployment problem, based on more concrete facts and being more accurate.

3. LABOR-SUPPLY PERSPECTIVE OF YOUTH UNEMPLOYMENT ANALYSIS

3.1 Two perspectives of analyzing youth unemployment problem

The rising of youth unemployment rate (or equally, the burst out of youth unemployment crisis) means large amount of youth having no jobs, the key issue of which is that many job seekers couldn't get employment, even though they are able to work and are actively seeking work. To analyze this problem, there are theoretically two perspectives to focus on: one is from the perspective of labor demand, considering a lack of job positions as the main reason and try to create more job opportunities; the other is from the perspective of labor supply, considering a lack of competencies of young job seekers as the key reason and try to help the youth become more competent.

Currently, researches and studies on youth unemployment problem have largely focused on the former one, which is to find out reasons of youth unemployment from the weakened economy and reduced labor demand and try to propose mechanisms to create enough job positions for the unemployed youth.

Based on whether or not the quality of employment[i] is taken into consideration, the perspective of labor demand could then be further divided into two directions. One focuses on the amount of job positions available for the youth and tries to provide more jobs—as long as there are jobs, and there is no differentiation between the level of jobs and quality of them. The second one pays attention to the quality of jobs provided and hopes to create enough "good" jobs for the youth, which may help the youth to build a proper set of skills and thus guarantee employment from a long-term point of view. This second aspect reflects a concern that is prevailing among certain group of unemployed youth, especially those who have received tertiary education, that turning down job offers with limited career prospect—which they believe they are "over-qualified" for and thus below their expectations.

---

[i] Relating to issues such as underemployment

Actions from labor-demand perspective dominate remedy measures that have been carried out, since those unemployed youth need jobs urgently. However, just as mentioned earlier in this book, there is a key question which is to distinguish between bringing down youth unemployment rate this time with the generalized question of youth unemployment problem. Justification of actions from labor-demand aspect is largely driven by the current situation—youth unemployment crisis we're currently experiencing, and when we neglect current situation, would the proposed mechanisms still be helpful and effective? Our reactions about youth unemployment problem have limited implications in the future, since there is no clue that they would help prevent youth unemployment crisis from recurring, and thus even though dealing with current youth unemployment crisis is of top priority, there is still a need to analyze the generalized youth unemployment problem, especially for researchers who are curious about youth unemployment.

When taking a long-term perspective to analyze youth unemployment problem, whether be caring about the long-term implication of current mechanisms (such as project Youth Guarantee) or trying to prevent youth unemployment crisis from recurring in the future, analysis from the perspective of labor-supply becomes particularly valuable. This is because the core of youth unemployment issue is the employment situation of young people, which could also be regarded as the living status of the youth. To help the youth, rather than relying on external factors such as a prosperous economy, a more reliable solution is to make the youth become more competent, since the status of economy changes so quickly and frequently that it can hardly be counted on.

To analyze youth unemployment problem from the perspective of labor supply, we focus on the competence of young people to explore the causes of youth unemployment problem and try to propose arrangements to help the youth build skills so as to better prepare them for employment. One branch of analysis from labor-supply perspective emphasizes on the revising and improving of education system. But we know this is not enough since there are so many youths who are out of school and couldn't benefit from the revising of education system. When taking into consideration the fact that the group of youth who have only received some basic level of education tends to have a higher youth unemployment rate, the value of revising education system is further reduced since those who are out of school constitute a larger part of the total youth who need help.

When we lay too much emphasize on labor demand, we may get lost in our effort to help the youth, since the core question of youth unemployment is not the number of jobs, but the youth, which is actually a labor-supply issue. In fact, when we move a step further, we find that our worry of youth unemployment crisis is not focusing on whether or not they have jobs, but on the living status and prospect of the youth. This is the ultimate reason that we care about youth unemployment crisis, and this is the ultimate concern of youth unemployment problem: the future of the youth.

When it comes to talking about the future of the youth, we simply cannot tell the younger generation that their future relies on external environment, which means they will have no jobs when the economy is bad, and they will have jobs when the economy is good. Also, we cannot say that being unemployed for a certain period of time will certainly means a gloomy future, since this is not the right thing to tell individuals. For the purpose of analyzing youth unemployment issues, we may say bad economy has driven up youth unemployment rate, but in front of a young guy, we would rather say that at any time, the future of an individual relates more to himself rather than his environment, or his work, and this is true even from the aspect of building of skills.

Generally speaking, it is true that working skills need to be developed through engaging in real work, which means if one wants to develop certain skills, he must first have a job. However, having no jobs doesn't necessarily mean that the youth couldn't develop skills or lack of competencies in the future. For example, a young person takes a gap year to travel around the world would be by definition considered as NEETs, since he is not in education, employment or training. However, there is no need for us to worry about this guy if he is clear about his situation and he is developing other skills through his journey.

We are confident that he will get a proper job when he finishes his touring and there is no reason for us to worry about his "unemployment". Examples from a contradictory standpoint may make this clearer—as Balzac, one famous French novelist once said, misfortune is a stepping-stone for the genius, a wealth for the capable and an abyss for the weak. J.K. Rowling has spent several years living on social welfare before the publication of her fiction, *Harry Potter and The Sorcerer's Stone*, and Ang Lee has spent more than 6 years living on his wife's support before his success as a film director. When we look back at their life paths, we may not feel pity for their experience of 'unemployment', since their huge achievements later in life have greatly benefited from that period of time.

The varieties of each person's life may make us miss the point if we focus on labor-demand perspective in the analysis of youth unemployment, since each unemployed youth is in different condition and is faced with different opportunities. To analyze from the perspective of labor supply, by examining the competencies of the youth, we may have the chance to better target at those who really need help and understand what kind of help they need. This book states that from the perspective of labor supply, the determinant factor of youth unemployment is the competencies of the youth, and external factors, such as conditions of the economy, mainly play a role like that of catalyst in a chemical reaction process. Whether chemical reaction will happen between two or more materials depends on the nature of materials involved in the reaction, rather than catalyst, and the role of catalyst is only to accelerate the process which already exists.

While an examination of the relationship between education and employment is a good start of analysis from labor-supply perspective, it is not enough. We need to explore more from the side of labor supply and go through more facts behind the phenomenon of rising youth unemployment rate.

3.2 Lack of skills also matters

Recall that in section 2.2, I introduce a piece of news on The Telegraph that many apprentice applicants are considered as unemployable for their lack of awareness of their responsibility towards the corporate sponsors[48]. In this case, young people themselves also play a role in their unemployment and what's their role in a broader issue—for instance, this youth unemployment crisis?

This is a tough question that requires tremendous efforts to answer. Luckily, to serve the need of understanding youth unemployment crisis from the perspective of education-to-employment process[i], McKinsey Center for Government (MCG) conducted a global survey across nine countries from August to September 2012. These nine countries included were Brazil, Germany, India, Mexico, Morocco, Saudi Arabia, Turkey, the United Kingdom and the United States, which were chosen "to provide a diverse set of geographies, labor markets and educational contexts". According to their report, this global survey consisted of three parallel questionnaires for the youth, employers and education providers, and the expected sample size for each country are 500 youths, 300 employers, and 100 education providers respectively, which constitute a total of 4,500 youth, 2,700 employers and 900 education

---

[i] To discuss the role of education in the occurring of large-scale youth unemployment crisis

providers across the nine countries in the survey.

For each of the three stakeholders surveyed, MCG had also paid attention to the diversity of the sample[49], so as to improve the representatives of survey result. The youth surveyed were aged between 15 and 29 and at the moment of being surveyed, they were either within the labor force or studying but would look for employment in 6 months. Based on their educational levels, these surveyed youths were further classified into five groups: less than high school, high school, vocational education, college or associate degrees and college/university degrees, and each education level had relatively equal number of people. Employers surveyed had a relatively broader representation of each business sector and different company size (small, medium and large), with manufacturing, wholesale and retail trade taking the largest proportion (19% and 17% respectively). Educational institutions surveyed covered open-access public institutions, selective public institutions, for-profit private institutions and not-for-profit private institutions.

Besides, due to the fact that Europe was hit badly by youth unemployment crisis this time, in order to understand the situation of Europe, MCG had also conducted a second survey using the same methodology as they did in 2012, lasting from August to September 2013, and covering six European countries: France, Greece, Italy, Portugal, Spain and Sweden. When they wrote their second report, except for results of this second survey, they also included data of Great Britain and Germany, which came from their first survey conducted in 2012.

These two surveys and their corresponding reports provide helpful insights into the fundamental facts behind this global youth unemployment crisis, and their value extends far beyond the original purpose of MCG's carrying out these surveys, which is to build a base of empirical fact under the framework of education to employment process. Here in my book, I will use some results of MCG's surveys that are presented in their reports, both for coming up with explanations of reasons of youth unemployment problem and for validating the soundness of explanations proposed—of course, I will not use the same fact both for proposition purpose and validation purpose.

Right now, this section won't illustrate contents of the two reports into detail, and readers could find the two reports titled *Education to Employment: Designing A System that Works* and *Education to Employment: Getting Europe's Youth into Work*[50] on the website of McKinsey. Here I will focus on one question: whether a lack of skills has prevented many youths from obtaining jobs, or equally, whether there are significant number of jobs that are not obtained by the youth even though they could get access to. When we figure out this question, we would understand whether or not the youth should also be responsible for their unemployment.

In the global survey of MCG, employers were asked, "Roughly how many vacant full-time entry level jobs does your company currently have?" And the averaged responds for large companies, medium companies and small companies are 27, 13 and 3 respectively[51]. This means a significant number of entry-level job vacancies exists, even for the periods following financial crisis. Besides, according to the result of MCG's first survey, roughly 43% employer respondents said they could recruit enough qualified entry-level candidates[52], and on average, 39% employers responded that a lack of skills was a common reason for entry-level job vacancies, with the specific number ranging from as high as 56% in Turkey and as low as 12% in Morocco.[53] Generally speaking, a majority of employers surveyed stated that young job seekers were not adequately prepared when they were searching and applying for jobs[54].

I will not exhibit the full result of MCG's global surveys, which readers could find easily on their website, and the purpose of this section is to use the result of their surveys to confirm the idea that there are many job opportunities which haven't been taken up by the youth and one key reason for this is the youth's lack of skills, or equally, youths' not well prepared. As a result, there is a great necessity to analyze youth unemployment problem from the perspective of labor supply: instead of discussing a lack of job opportunities, discusses the lack of skills.

3.3 One-stakeholder approach of youth unemployment analysis

Researches about youth unemployment problem have generally followed a multi-stakeholder approach, which means to analyze the ultimate cause of youth unemployment crisis by examining the roles of different stakeholders and their interactions, which typically include employers, education providers, policy makers, macroeconomic situations and young people themselves. The analysis from labor-demand perspective is in nature a multi-stakeholder approach, since it includes at least two stakeholders—young people and the employers, not to mention that in most cases, macroeconomic conditions of certain country involved would also be taken into consideration.

Right now, the majority of researches from labor-supply perspective have also take a multi-stakeholder approach, as is shown in MCG's two reports I mentioned previously, which try to build an education-to-employment highway and connect employers and young people through education providers. Or another book on youth unemployment, *Generation Jobless? Turning the Youth Unemployment Crisis into Opportunity*[55], in which professor Vogel (2015) specifically highlights the approach of taking a multi-stakeholder approach in his analysis.

Different from approaches mentioned above, this book tries to analyze the causes of youth unemployment problem following a one-stakeholder approach. Specifically, this book focuses on the youth themselves to explore the causes of youth unemployment problem, in which there is only one stakeholder—young people. Even though corresponding solutions suggested later will inevitably involve various stakeholders, this doesn't change the fact that it follows the one-stakeholder approach, since whatever solutions are proposed based on the needs to change one thing, other things would be affected more or less, directly or indirectly. This book tries to analyze the reasons of youth unemployment problem from the unemployed youth, which means to treat youth unemployment problem as the problem of young people, not that of other stakeholders, and youth unemployment crisis occurs for reasons of the youth, not other stakeholders too. If, on the contrary, several stakeholders are identified as the causes of youth unemployment crisis, then all these stakeholders need change in order to help the unemployed youth.

Figure 3.1 and figure 3.2 exhibit the difference between a one-stakeholder approach and a multi-stakeholder approach, even if all these two approaches take a perspective of labor-supply.

Labor-supply perspective of youth unemployment analysis

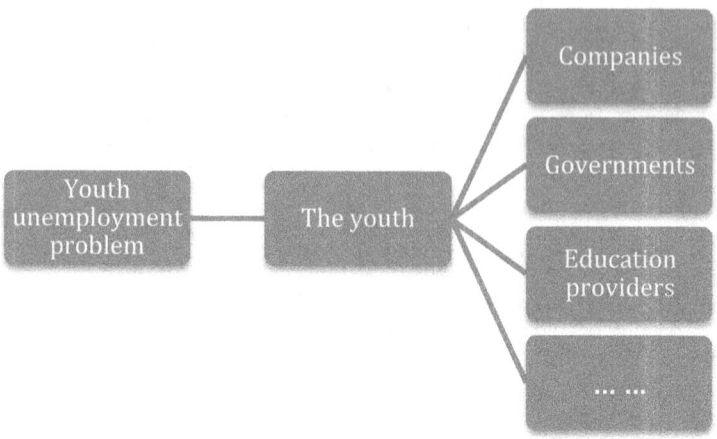

Figure 3.1 An analysis of the causes of youth unemployment problem following one-stakeholder approach

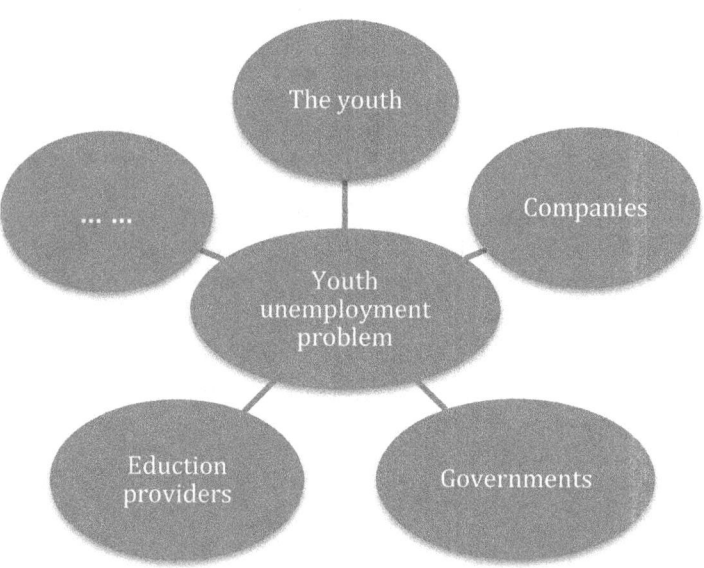

Figure 3.2 An analysis of the causes of youth unemployment problem following multi-stakeholder approach

From figure 3.1, we could easily identify the characteristic of one-stakeholder approach: first identifies the youth as the cause of youth unemployment problem, and then tries to find how to change the youth. By comparing figure 3.1 with figure 3.2, we would find that the key difference between a one-stakeholder approach and a multi-stakeholder one is that the former considers youth unemployment as the problem of the youth, and other stakeholders such as on-site training providers or educational institutions get involved in the discussion of youth unemployment through their impact on the youth. For a multi-stakeholder approach, various stakeholders are connected with the occurring of youth unemployment problem directly, without the mediator of the youth, and this means a multi-stakeholder approach believes other stakeholders besides the youth should also be responsible for the occurring of youth unemployment crisis.

The analysis of this book bases on the fact that there are significant number of entry-level job positions available for young people yet not taken up by them, and many of them fail to obtain these jobs for their lack of competencies deemed by employers. In order to figure out whether this is justified, I focus on the analysis of recruitment. The method of taking recruitment as the target could be considered as a circuit, which constitutes a complete system to analyze youth unemployment: if one could pass recruitment process successfully, he has no unemployment problem, and when each youth makes it, there is no youth unemployment problem; on the contrary, if large amount of youth couldn't pass the recruitment process, they don't have jobs and there comes youth unemployment problem.

In the analysis of recruitment, one side is the youth with supply of labor, and the other side is employers with demand of labor, and if the youth fulfill the requirements set by recruiters, they will get jobs whatever macroeconomic conditions are[i]. As a result, this focus of recruitment could be considered as a small-scale yet completed analysis of the cause of youth unemployment, since when young people pass recruitment, there is no youth unemployment problem, otherwise there is, and thus, to understand the occurring of youth unemployment problem is equal to understand why many youths couldn't pass recruitment.

One thing needs to be clarified here that the analysis of recruitment still consists of two stakeholders: the youth and the employers, or equivalently, the competences of young people and the recruitment requirements of employers. But this won't constitute a problem and the analysis of recruitment would be converted to a one-stakeholder

---

[i] Under the fact that there is a significant number of job vacancies even during this latest youth unemployment crisis

analysis if we consider the recruitment requirements of employers to be constant and only the competence of the youth is a changeable variable: with employers' requirements given constant, only competence of the youth needs to be analyzed, since this is the only changeable variable.

To assume recruitment requirements as constant doesn't mean that they won't change, since we could easily provide counterexamples such as computer skills, which didn't gain much popularity in the workplace two decades ago. And recently, data science and machine learning skills have been favored by more and more employers, which haven't been so several years ago. In fact, the actual meaning of stating recruitment requirements to be constant is just to exclude it from the discussion of youth unemployment problem, or in other words, we accept what they are and no matter how much they've changed, all job seekers could do is to cater to these changes, rather than ask them to change back.

3.4 The necessities of one-stakeholder analysis (1)

To analyze youth unemployment problem from the perspective of labor-supply, we could take two approaches: the one-stakeholder approach and the multi-stakeholder approach. Currently, nearly all researches have used a multi-stakeholder approach, but right now, I will verify the importance of one-stakeholder approach: it is not only a supplementary analysis to the commonly-used multi-stakeholder approach, but also a necessary one.

This could be understood through three aspects: firstly, beyond youth unemployment rate, there is a need to explore more about the situation that young people are experiencing; secondly, while external factors such as the economic condition does play a role, we cannot count on it for its high uncertainties; thirdly, to analyze following a multi-stakeholder approach will bring about barriers when it comes to the stage of proposing solutions. I will illustrate these three points one by one, with the first two illustrated in this section.

(1) Beyond youth unemployment rate, there are much more that need to be examined for the purpose of understanding the situation that young people are experiencing.

Figures, including youth unemployment rate, are only indicators of young people's employment situation. For youth unemployment rate, it just pays attention to whether or not young people have jobs, but as we all know, people's employment status and career prospect is more than having jobs or not. Focusing too much on unemployment rate will naturally make us neglect other fundamental facts, which when neglected, might be misleading for truly conquering youth unemployment problem.

On one hand, the quality of employment is likely worse than we have expected. In October 2012, an article[56] from The Guardian related data from a report prepared by OECD, which stated that across 16 member states of EU, number of young people engaged in employment reached a historical low level and for those employed, their jobs are less secure with fewer working hours. And in 2011, "42% of young working Europeans were in temporary employment," with nearly 30% young adults in part-time employment, levels both increased significantly compared with a decade ago. On the other hand, many youths have dropped out of labor force, whether due to a lack of skills or a lack of ambition. Those who have dropped out of labor force may suffer from everlasting unemployment and thus become a huge burden for the society. Yet this group of youths won't be included in our examination when we follow a labor-demand approach and just hope to lower down youth unemployment rate, since they are not included in the calculation of youth unemployment rate[i]. And we must be aware that when this group of youths are taken into consideration, the situation that our society is faced with would be actually worse than the situation indicated by a rising youth unemployment rate.

Besides, when analyze the impact of youth unemployment crisis, many researches have pointed out the probably adverse effect to the unemployed youth and the society, not only relating to the development of economy, but also relating to young people's welfare as human beings. We are worried about the harmful effect of unemployment to the growth of human being, and we acknowledge that people's skills cannot be built in one day. Thus, in order to get a comprehensive view of young people's employment prospect, there is definitely a need to examine more about the status of the youth, since just as I have discussed before, the information revealed by youth unemployment rate is really limited.

(2) While external factors such as macroeconomic condition does play a role, we cannot count on it for its high uncertainties.

As we all know, there exist business cycles and each country as well as the whole world experience business circles periodically. This time, the

---

[i] When they have dropped out of labor force, they will not get included in the calculation of labor force, which is the denominator when calculates youth unemployment rate

2008 financial crisis has weakened the global economy, reduced labor demand and then enlarged the scale of youth unemployment crisis. And in history, there were many times when economic downturn caused by expected or unexpected factors drove up unemployment rate (and possibly youth unemployment rate). How could we guarantee that there won't be such factors in the future? Could we confidently state that economic conditions would remain stable all the time? Certainly not.

What if weak demand of labor caused by a weakened economy happens again? Would our methods of creating jobs to help the unemployed youth be able to be applied to the new crisis then? Largely not, since labor conditions, economic conditions and other factors will all be different from today—not to mention the effectiveness of current methods still remains obscure.

Highly uncertain as the global economy or the economic condition of one specific country is, high price will we pay once economic environment worsens. People may say that the world and real life are always unpredictable, yet our human society still progresses successfully and continuously, and the level of human civilization is much higher than what it was hundreds of years ago, or even decades ago. While this is true, we must be aware that even though as a country or our human society as a whole, we could handle the suddenly burst out of youth unemployment crisis, those young individuals involved may not be able to cope well, especially during their first attempt of entering job market. Experiencing unemployment in a young age may be too severe a setback for individuals to deal with.

As mentioned earlier, many researches have studied the long-term adverse effects caused by unemployment in a young age, and their findings show that these adverse effects might be permanent and irreversible in certain conditions. What makes this situation worse is that many youths may simply drop out of labor force when they fail to enter job market successfully and this is exactly what once happened in Japan. The Financial Times published an article[57] by Robin Harding, *titled New World of Work: Japan's Lost Generation Struggles to Catch Up*, in which the author states that "Japan's 1990 stock market crash has led large amount of Japanese drop out of labor force, and there are 340,000 Japanese men aged between 35 to 44 dropping out of labor force, doubled since 20 years ago." What would those youth live on when they have no jobs during their lifetime?

When we focus too much on the side of labor-demand, we will miss the group of youths who have dropped out of labor force, since they are excluded in the calculation of youth unemployment rate. And when we rely too much on external factors, young people will suffer once external conditions weaken again. For those individuals who cannot handle such problem, the cost to them may be too huge to bear, and when the number of youths under this situation accumulates, the society as a whole would have to confront this accumulated pressure directly.

The world has become much "flatter" than before, and the flow of labor force will forever increase competition in labor market in each corner of the world. This is a trend that one cannot deny, which would further reinforce the pressure that the youth must undertake for competing in labor market. As a result, young people must prepare well for their employment.

3.5 The necessities of one-stakeholder analysis (2)

There is a third reason that makes the one-stakeholder analysis valuable, a reason that is more practical and pressing than the first two. This third reason is that to analyze youth unemployment problem following a multi-stakeholder approach will naturally bring out barriers when it comes to the stage of proposing solutions.

Governments' policies, companies' training programs or educational systems are set up for various considerations, and if they are altered just for reasons of the unemployed youth, benefits of other stakeholders will be affected, which may lead to a more harmful situation than that lead by youth unemployment problem. If young people's employment issue wasn't included in the debate of formation of the original policies or training programs—which means young people's employment issue is of less importance for these policies or programs compared with other stakeholders, the change of these policies or programs just for the purpose of helping the youth won't make much sense. In fact, when more stakeholders get involved in one discussion, difficulties of reaching consensus will increase. And when too many stakeholders are involved, there may even be unable to reach a consensus since the benefits of each stakeholder will get intertangled with each other, and a small change to one clause may alter the benefits of other stakeholders significantly.

As a result, when we follow a multi-stakeholder approach to analyze youth unemployment problem, it will be less likely to achieve *Pareto Improvement*, which means while increasing the welfare of young people, benefits of other stakeholders won't get harmed. When many policies need to be altered, other stakeholders besides the youth will inevitably be affected, which causes huge difficulty for achieving Pareto Improvement. Even if there is room for Pareto Improvement, searching for clues, making a proposal, reaching consensus and finally carrying out the desired plan might be too time-consuming as well as costly to perform, and this favors one-stakeholder approach over the multi-stakeholder one, since a one-stakeholder approach would reduce potential influences on other stakeholders to the great extent.

Let's have a look at one simplified example.

In winter, the air-conditioner is functioning to keep the classroom warm, which is set under the request of students who feel cold. Later, some visitors enter, and they feel hot since they wear too much, and shortly after coming in, they ask for turning off the air-conditioner. Should the air-conditioner be turned off under the new request? Largely not, otherwise some students might get cold. The air-conditioner is turned on for one group of people—the students and should not be turned off just for needs of another group of people—the visitors, and this is a typical dilemma that would be included in any analysis following a multi-stakeholder approach. If we solve this case follow a one-stakeholder approach, we would identify those visitors as the cause of their feeling hot, and they should take off some clothes. If they still feel hot, then they could discuss with the students who feel cold and try to turn down the temperature of the air-conditioner to a suitable level, or even turn it off.

In this simplified case, we have solved the problem following a-one stakeholder approach. However, people may question that following a multi-stakeholder approach, they could also solve the problem. For example, let the new comers take off some clothes and meantime, lower down the temperature of the air-conditioner to a level acceptable for both groups of people. While it is acceptable and practical for this case, it is still different from a one-stakeholder approach since in a one-stakeholder approach, the visitors are considered as the stakeholder who should be responsible for the temperature issue, and they should change as much as they can in order to fit in, while the changes of other stakeholders, if there is any, just depends. Following the one-stakeholder approach, the changes of other stakeholders will be reduced to the minimum level, which would make them more willing to accept those changes. If at the very beginning—as we would when follow a multi-stakeholder approach, we identify both the new comers and students in the classroom are responsible for the new comers' feeling hot, how many clothes should new comers take off and which temperature should the air-conditioner be set then? There comes puzzle and confusion and there is high possibility that the students who feel cold would disagree with the turning down of temperature.

This case is just a simplified example used for illustration purpose, which doesn't mean that the needs of students should be prioritized than the needs of visitors. The decided temporary of air-conditioner is like a policy or arrangement that has been implemented, and the students in the classroom are like the stakeholders whose benefits have been properly addressed in the formation of the policy or arrangement. And visitors' asking for turning off the air-conditioner is like to change one policy for the interests of a new stakeholder, whose benefits have been originally neglected or considered less of concern during the debate of formation of the established policy.

The key message conveyed by this example is that, no matter how well a multi-stakeholder approach works, the changes and efforts required will be much greater than a one-stakeholder approach, not to mention whether or not they could choose a proper arrangement to balance the benefits of various stakeholders. The result is that solutions proposed following a multi-stakeholder approach will face stronger resistance and cost more than a one-stakeholder approach, which may even lead to the stagnation of proper action[i]. This difficulty is concrete and must get included in the discussion of youth unemployment problem following a multi-stakeholder approach.

1) Education systems

To help the youth, reform of education system has also been emphasized, especially for some research institutions. For example, in the report *Education to Employment: Designing A System that Works*, the authors exhibit their survey result showing that more than one half of surveyed youths value hands-on training as especially effective, yet they have received inadequate training in such manner.[58] And they propose the reform of education providers to better cooperate with companies to serve the employment needs of young people.

However, there are many educators who highlight liberal education, which they believe matters more than specific skills for graduates' career. And, there is already a separation of occupational training and academic training in many countries' education system, such as that of Germany. When we realize that even though the number of unemployed youths is large, their number is still much smaller than that of those who are employed, and if we alter education system dramatically just because a

---

[i] Remember that policy makers will have to spend months or even years in order to implement a change in certain policies

relatively small number of youths cannot find jobs, the prospect of the larger group of youths will be affected and unpredictable risks may arise, which may be too costly for us to bear. Apparently, the revising of education system needs a detailed investigation and a through discussion, which may take a longer period of time than we've expected.

2) Companies

Companies have been encouraged to provide more trainee positions to the youth, but just as has been discussed, the number of job positions in a company is determined by internal needs and external environment of the company, which has nothing to do with the number of unemployed youths. The priority for entrepreneurs' setting up firms is generally to make profits and doesn't relate to allocate people to work, which is typically the mission of a government agency or a social welfare institution. As a result, to urge the creation of large number of trainee positions in firms may simply go contrary to the benefits of these firms, and this is a question that especially matters for firms that are shorting of competitive advantage in the market.

Companies have reasons to worry, and their worries make sense. For example, it is generally recognized that there is a relatively high turnover rate among young people, since the youth used to try many different sorts of jobs before they are willing to settle down. Based on this consideration, it is unwise for certain firms to invest a lot in young people, since they may just leave the firm shortly after these training periods end. Weak firms couldn't compete with big firms in attracting talents, and they are also more sensitive to young people's turnover rate since the number of employees they have used to be smaller and they have a much lower tolerance of ineffective investment. In fact, companies are easy to fall into bankruptcy, and how could companies set aside resources to help young people when they cannot take care of themselves?

Under this situation, governments' command of firms recruiting more youths for social welfare purpose goes contrary to the benefits of these firms, and this is why funds from government is needed badly for this kind of arrangement. In fact, many apprenticeship programs provided by firms are essentially that the government buys these programs and training opportunities from firms and then give them to the youth, with the funds from government being used to cover the cost of firms' training programs. It is no wonder that once government fund is cut down, training positions will decrease instantly. Remember I have related contents from an article titled *Small Firms Warn Funding Cuts May Stop the Boom in Apprentice Jobs in Its Tracks and Hit Young Workers*, which reveals the reaction of firms for government fund cutting down: reduce number or simply cease apprenticeship programs.

3) Government policies

One focus from the aspect of government policies targets at the minimum wage policy, which many people believe have excluded youth from getting employment since the youth are typically low-skilled and only deserve relatively lower salary under market conditions. Suppose this conclusion is true, could we then reduce the level of minimum wage or even abolish this minimum wage policy? Perhaps not, at least not just for the reason of youth unemployment.

The original purpose of setting up minimum wage has nothing to do with whether young people could find jobs or not, but to protect those who have jobs and to guarantee them a certain life standard. Once level of minimum wage is reduced or the policy being abolished, benefits of current employees will be badly harmed. As a result, even though we recognize minimum wage policy might possibly drive up youth unemployment rate, we can hardly change it in short-term, since it requires a careful and prolonged investigation and negotiation. The same is true for the discussion of immigration policy or free trade policy in the formation of youth unemployment crisis.

Government policy will have significant impact over various stakeholders and the change of any policy will alter benefits of those stakeholders in different ways. Then, a time-consuming and costly investigation would be needed theoretically for any change. The problem of a multi-stakeholder approach is that the proposal of solutions requires a time-consuming investigation and discussion, which may even be impossible to conduct when it comes to the discussion of revising education system, since their consequences may only appear half a century later.

This is where one-stakeholder approach helps. Following this approach, youth unemployment problem is considered as problem of the youth, not others. And the youth are responsible for tackling the problem to a great extent, while other stakeholders just play a supplementary and occasional role. In this way, conflicts between the youth and other stakeholders that arise from helping young people getting jobs will get addressed properly, and the following solutions are much likely to be implemented successfully.

Frankly speaking, it's still open to discussion that whether there exist severe conflicts of interests between young people and other stakeholders in young people's unemployment issue, but this does not make it easier for other stakeholders to help the youth. For example, it is noticed that when the economy is in recession, youth unemployment rate tends to rise, and when we apply a multi-stakeholder method to help the youth, the society needs to provide more jobs for young people. However, we know that during a recession, demand is weak and so is the production of society, which means there is fewer job openings and fiscal revenue tends to fall, and in this case, how could the debt-laden government, as well as struggling companies to allocate additional resources to help the youth? Aid from other stakeholders must get cut when it is needed most, this is somewhat confusing and counterintuitive, since the unemployed youths benefit little from what we've found. As a result, we cannot be satisfied with current knowledge about youth unemployment, and we must move on.

In order to fully understand youth unemployment problem and conquer it, we need a further analysis of the situation of young people, since our current knowledge hasn't told us all that we need. Besides, we cannot count on external factors due to their uncertainties and a multi-stakeholder approach may not be sustainable or be too costly to achieve. The conclusion is that even if one-stakeholder approach will not replace the multi-stakeholder approach, it is a useful supplementary to the commonly used multi-stakeholder method. And later in this book, when I state that "to analyze youth unemployment from the perspective of labor supply", I actually mean "to analyze youth unemployment from the perspective of labor supply and use the one-stakeholder approach".

3.6 The focus and assumptions of my analysis

In this section, I'll introduce the topic of my analysis, methodology used and the assumptions.

1) My topic

In this book, the core is the youth. Should young people be responsible for their unemployment?

There are actually two topics in my analysis, with one following the other. The first topic is to analyze causes of youth unemployment problem from the perspective of labor-supply, and specifically, this question is whether young people are competent enough for employment. The second topic is that if the youth are not considered as competent by employers, what are the reasons and how could they improve their competencies.

2) My methodology

The methodology used to answer the first topic is to focus on recruitment, with the first step being to propose a highly summarized framework illustrating the requirements of recruitment. And the second step is to analyze facts gathered about youth labor force under the recruitment framework introduced in the first step.

Facts used in this analysis come from three sources, with the most important one being the results of McKinsey's two global surveys mentioned before. And the latter two sources of facts include my personal experience, both of my own experience and my observation of the experience of other people, and information as well as discussions that I read from the Internet.

As readers would notice in following chapters of my book, I've used plenty of data that are presented in McKinsey's reports, and many crucial ideas that I put forward later in my book are proposed based on their data. This is partly because, as I've suggested previously and as is mentioned in McKinsey's reports, that youth unemployment is relatively a new topic and "existing data is limited and cannot be compared across countries". While McKinsey's empirical fact base is built focusing on the journey from education to employment, it does provide valuable facts. Facts could be explained from different perspectives and then their data constitute the foundation of my analysis following my logic. In fact, it is acceptable to state that without their data, I won't be able to conduct my research, not to mention to write this book.

3) The Assumptions

There are there assumptions of my analysis and let me introduce these three assumptions one by one.

Assumption 1: there is a significant number of job opportunities that are not taken up by the youth.

The value of my whole analysis is based on the belief that while youth unemployment rate is high, there is large number of entry-level job vacancies exist. This means this book doesn't pay attention to the part of youth unemployment happened due to an excess of labor supply compared with labor demand. Luckily, this assumption is supported by real world evidence, which is particularly reflected in the results of McKinsey' global surveys.

The analysis of recruitment in this study is a kind of static analysis, with an implicit and embedded assumption that the unemployed youth could get access to those entry-level job vacancies, and the reason of there existing job vacancies is that the youth fail to meet requirements of these jobs. People may ask that to understand the formation of natural rate of unemployment, economists have proposed concepts like frictional unemployment and structural unemployment, with frictional unemployment referring to the formation of unemployment due to not being able to get access to suited job opportunities. And now, I state that there is a significant number of job opportunities that are not taken up by the youth, what if this happens because young people cannot get access to these job openings?

If the youth cannot get access to these opportunities due to the distance factor for example (such as the area where certain group of young people live has no companies with job openings), our corresponding solution would be trying to help the youth reach out to these companies, rather than examining the incompetence of the youth. However, as we would find from McKinsey's survey and facts I gathered from the Internet, employers do provide their opinions about young job seekers or their newly recruited employees, and this means employers get access to young applicants, which also means young applicants do get access to job opportunities…yet be rejected by recruiters. And then, this first assumption is reasonable.

One question about this assumption is that have young people's employment status of taking temporary positions or dropping out of labor force been included in this one-stakeholder analysis? I would say yes. This is because situations like underemployment and dropping out of labor force are considered as comparatively worse situation than proper employment, and under assumption 1, this means that the youth in these two kinds of situation did not obtain their desired job positions. Then, my analysis will contribute to the understanding of their underemployment or dropping out of labor force.

Assumption 2: when examining whether the youth are qualified for employment, there is only one variable, which is the youth, and all other factors presume to be constant.

This assumption relates to the method of analysis: focusing on recruitment. To be specific, there are at least two factors that are considered as constant, with the first one being the recruitment criteria used by employers in recruitment process, and the second being the macroeconomic conditions. My one-stakeholder analysis relies on analysis of recruitment, and only when recruitment requirement of recruiters remain constant, would it be possible to examine the status on the side of labor supply. If recruitment criteria are not constant, then to match two sides of the recruitment process, there are two variables that could change: the skills of the youth and the requirements of the employers, which would significantly increase the complexity of analysis. Luckily, as I have illustrated before, the assumption that recruitment requirement remaining constant makes sense.

Assumption 3: the reasons of youth unemployment do not vary much among different countries.

In reality, different countries have different characteristics and arrangements, which would affect youth unemployment situation considerably. However, recognizing those differences among different countries belongs to the multi-stakeholder approach and complicates the solving of youth unemployment problem, and thus neglecting these factors—differences among different countries—when examining whether the youth should also be responsible for their unemployment, is a rational and practical choice. In fact, as will be revealed later in this book, the growth path of children in different countries is similar, which is based on the fundamental basis that we are all human beings. Children's growth path is similar and so is their journey towards a fruitful career: for example, whichever country it is, young people will have to pass recruitment in order to get jobs. As a result, assumption 3 is also reasonable.

One implication of hypothesis 3 in my analysis is that during the introduction and illustration of necessities and the importance of one-stakeholder approach in youth unemployment analysis, I have used cases from different countries in different parts of my logic line. For example, I use cases in the UK to illustrate the relative unsustainability of governmental-funded apprenticeships and use cases in Japan to present the serious consequences of unable to get employed during young people's first attempt of entering job market, and I further use data of the US's 50 states to illustrate the relationship between age and youth unemployment rate.

To conduct analysis in this way, I assume that governmental-funded apprenticeship in Japan—if there is any—would face the same difficulty as that has appeared in the UK and young people in the UK would experience similar trouble as young people in Japan when they fail to enter job market successfully. And for European countries or Asian countries, the older of young people tend to have lower rate of youth unemployment compared with the younger ones, just as is shown by data of the UA. This may not be exactly true but is relatively sound because this book aims to analyze youth unemployment from a normalized perspective—focusing on youths themselves, and the growth path of youths in each country is the same—because we are all humans.

Part B: The analysis of youth unemployment problem

4. THE RECRUITMENT FORMULA

4.1 Recruitment: the starting point of understanding youth unemployment

To understand youth unemployment problem from the perspective of labor supply, recruitment is the starting point.

As we often read from the advertisements of recruitment, there is a factor relating to university degree, and it would be better if it is obtained from a "well-known" institute. What if a candidate has no chance to be considered just because he doesn't possess a university degree? This is a question that hasn't been included in the discussion of youth unemployment problem so far. The general ideas of the causes of youth unemployment problem focus on either a lack of job positions or a lack of skills, but in this case, there are job positions and the candidate may have the right set of skills, yet he is still unable to get the job.

How should we understand this phenomenon? Does it simply happen due to not possessing a university degree?

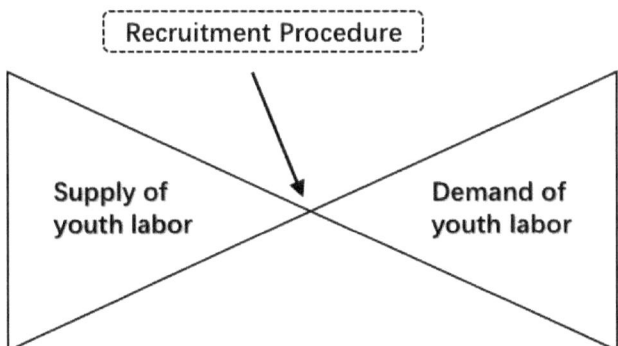

Figure 4.1 Recruitment connects two sides of youth labor

This book takes the perspective of labor supply and focuses on examining recruitment, which I believe is the starting point of exploring the reasons of youth unemployment problem. As is showing in figure 4.1, recruitment is right the procedure that links two sides of youth labor: supply of youth labor and demand of youth labor. If a young applicant passes the recruitment procedure organized by a company, he is employed, and on the contrary, if he cannot successfully pass all the recruitment procedures arranged by companies, he has no jobs. For this reason, the procedure of recruitment doesn't only connect the supply and demand of youth labor, but also two opposite situation that we are discussing about: employment and unemployment. When too many youths fail during recruitment procedure, youth unemployment rate rises and here comes the youth unemployment crisis.

Could we find clues of reasons of young people's failing to obtain jobs by analyzing recruitment procedure? I would say yes, and in fact, this is a necessary step for an analysis from labor-supply side. Consider questions like this: Would a guy who can speak more than ten languages but has no financial background gets a position in financial services industry? Would a young man facing competition from international students obtain a good job with generous salary? Or would a young lady get a job when macroeconomic conditions in her country isn't that good?

The answers for those questions are the same: we don't know. We don't know until he or she has taken part in recruitment procedures organized by companies, or we will never know the answer. If the first guy passes recruitment procedure successfully and gets an offer from a financial organization, we know that he could get a position in financial services industry even though he doesn't have a finance degree. If the lady passes recruitment procedures and gets an offer, we know she could still have a job even though the economy condition in her country is bad. So is another case: if he passes recruitment successfully and we instantly know that he could get jobs, even though the competition with international students has been tough. Or if they couldn't pass recruitment, we realize that they do not get those jobs. Noticing that getting employment through acquaintance or social network doesn't mean that there is no recruitment procedure or recruitment requirement, and even if specific procedures may vary, the core is the same: those who get employed through network must first fulfill the requirements of recruitment, otherwise the related companies will not hire them.

Let's understand the role of recruitment procedure by looking at the movement of sand in a sandglass. If the sand from one part passes through the joint in the middle, it moves to the other part, otherwise the sand stays in the original half of the sandglass. And for the youth, if they pass recruitment successfully, they have jobs, and if not, they then belong to the group of youths who are unemployed.

The key issue here is that recruitment connects two opposite status of young people: employed or unemployed. No matter how many factors would affect the employment status of young people, their impacts are reflected in their influences over recruitment, and the ultimate question of youth unemployment problem is whether the youth could pass recruitment procedure successfully, or equally whether the youth fulfill recruitment requirement of employers. Corporations recruit employees they need by organizing recruitment events and individuals apply for jobs by taking part in these recruitment events: this is the natural and normal behavior concerning labor demand and supply. Recruitment reflects the core relationship in youth labor market that should be analyzed for unemployment purpose and reflects the key difference between an employed youth and an unemployed one. As a result, to examine recruitment is the best way to understand whether the youth—that's the side of labor supply, should also be responsible for their unemployment problem.

The method that this book takes to examine recruitment is to summarize and conceptualize the recruitment requirements of employers and then test the competence of the youth under this conceptualized set of recruitment requirement. If competencies of the youth fulfill recruitment requirements of employers, they will get employed and there is no labor-supply issue of youth unemployment problem. Otherwise, if the youth do not fulfill requirements of recruitment, there is labor-supply issue of youth unemployment problem and then, we need explore further about why many youths fail to meet requirements of employers. I will use facts that I have gathered about young people as indicators of young people's competencies[i].

4.2 Recruitment Formula: definition

Currently, companies are placed at the center of youth unemployment discussion, and their arranging more training and apprenticeship positions are considered as the best way to deal with youth unemployment crisis. While this mechanism benefits the youth, it might not be consistent with interests of these companies. An example is that

---

[i] As has been illustrated in section 3.6, there are three sources of facts analyzed in this book: results of McKinsey's two global surveys, information read online, and my own experience as well as my observation

companies generally need external funds and support to carry out those training programs, and once external funds get cut, apprenticeship positions decrease. This indicates the incapability of some companies helping the youth, especially for smaller firms, since companies have to compete in the cruel business world. Under this acknowledgement, all their actions should be in favor of one goal—their survival and development, and if one action does not contribute to this goal, it should at least not go against that, otherwise rational companies will certainly refuse to take actions.

When will companies begin to recruit new employees? When there is a need of new members for their own benefits. While participating actively with education providers or policy makers to help the unemployed youth may bring good fame, these benefits may not be large enough to cover the cost that companies have to bear in order to support these projects. Besides, when it comes to recruit new employees, whether for formal position or intern positions, in general cases companies must be very careful about its recruitment process and make their decisions based on concrete criteria. Ideally, the need of recruitment must derive from the need of the company, whether it is to expand current businesses, open a new branch or launch a new product. All in all, companies recruit new employees because they need additional people to solve their own problems.

Once new employees are hired and get started to work, will companies' problems be solved quickly? Largely not, and companies have to wait for certain periods of time before those newly hired employees could make contributions. For example, newly recruited young people will, at least, spend some time understanding the operation of the firm and its businesses, through which process they learn and master the skills they need to perform their tasks. While at the early stage of being recruited young people might not bring in what their employers desire, they will certainly carry with them what employers do not desire—costs.

Young people do have some kinds of skills, but they still have to spend some time learning specific skills that they will use at their positions, or at least spend some time understanding the new environment and its culture. During this period of time, companies will typically have to arrange tutors to guide them and to tolerate some mistakes that they might make, which is certainly kind of a burden for these firms. And of course, companies have to pay the newly recruited young people salaries, which is also a cost from companies' perspective. Only when this period of time has passed by, and when the newly recruited have mastered their skills, would they bring more benefits to the firm than costs. As a result, there is a mismatch between benefits of new recruitment and costs of new recruitment from the perspective of companies: in the very beginning, benefits are relatively smaller than costs and later on, this relationship is expected to reverse.

This mismatch between benefits and costs brings about a consideration relating to the dimension of time. In the early days of entering a company, newly recruited youths will bring more costs than benefits to the company, and gradually, this relationship gets reversed. Thus, for a rational recruiter, he would only recruit a candidate if he believes the candidate will stay at his firm long enough so that the candidate would create more accumulated value for the firm than accumulated costs. If, on the contrary, the newly recruited employee just stays in the firm for a short period of time and then quits, this is definitely a loss from the company's standpoint.

Generally speaking, if newly recruited employees resign shortly after signing the contract, companies' long-term plan gets affected to some degree and they will have to recruit new staffs to fill the vacancies that those former employees left. Let's understand this by using the well-known Discount Cash Flow (DCF) model. DCF model is usually used to decide whether to invest in a business unit and if the present value of all streams of future net cash inflows is greater than the initial cost, companies will go into the investment. To apply DCF model to the analysis of recruitment, when companies lay emphasize on the future benefits of recruiting new employees, they will invest a lot to help those newly recruited to develop their skills, and if these newly recruited employees resign and work for other firms, the original firms will suffer a huge loss, not to mention the subsequent costs resulted from an interruption of certain business plan and the subsequent costs of arranging another event of recruitment. As a result, even if recruiters acknowledge that within a short period of time the benefits of recruiting someone is larger than the costs of this recruitment, they may still reject the candidate if they expect the candidate won't stay long in the firm.

To conclude, companies' decision about whether to recruit a new employee bases on the relationship between the benefits of recruiting additional employee and the relevant cost. If the company believes that the benefits of recruiting are larger than the costs, the company will likely give the candidate an offer, otherwise it will just turn down the application. Meantime, to complete analysis, this statement must be added with a requirement—that this inequation will hold in the long term. If the inequation is valid only in short term and does not hold for long term, the decision of recruiting is still a bad one and the company will likely not hire the new employee.

Up to now, the recruitment formula that I will use for further analysis is about to come out, and before that, I have to explain one potential confusion that the benefits and costs of recruiting a new employee refers to the potential outcome after the employee being hired, and thus the benefits and costs incurred before that time would not be included in the decision about whether hiring the candidate. For example, the benefits of social media coverage led by companies participating in cooperation with schools cannot be considered as benefits of recruitment, and the costs of arranging personnel to organize recruitment events and provide interviews cannot be considered as costs of recruitment. These sorts of benefits and costs, which occur before a specific employee being hired and are shared by all candidates, will not be taken into consideration when decide whether or not recruiting any individual candidate.

Recruitment Formula introduced in this book summaries the general rule that recruiters follow to decide whether or not hiring an applicant, and it is expressed as: *"Concerning the decision of whether hiring a candidate, from the standpoint of recruiters: If benefits of having the candidate as an employee is believed by the recruiter to be larger than relevant costs, and this inequation is believed by the recruiter to hold in the long run, the firm will hire the candidate."*

This is the Recruitment Formula that will be used to examine whether the youth—labor-supply side of youth labor force, should also be responsible for youth unemployment problem.

4.3 Benefits and costs of recruitment

In the former part, I propose a concept summarizing the general rule that employers follow to recruit new staff. Now let's see how this concept relates to employers' requirements towards job seekers: I'll deduce specific requirements of employers from this concept.
What are the benefits of recruiting a new employee?

Companies' recruiting new members starts from needs of their businesses, and the most obvious benefit of hiring a new staff is the continuity of daily operation of the company. New employee participates in the operation of the firm and maintains the normal business of that firm. For a manufacturer, the role of a new entry-level staff is about to operate machines to produce components or to join in the administration department and take a role as assistant of firm's operation, or what else. Meantime, a branch of a bank recruits a new teller to sit behind the glass wall to help clients who come to the bank for account-related service, a school recruits a new teacher to teach students English grammar, and a consulting firm recruits a business analyst to provide insights about the business environment and future trends in certain sectors. No matter what kind of role the newly hired will play, they will join a specific department and conduct a specific task. To do well of the job, to possess relevant skills is a must, whether it be hard skills like computer skills or soft skills like communication skills.

Besides company's daily operation, newly recruited employees may also bring in other benefits that companies desire, such as advanced technique and latest management knowledge, which may contribute to the innovation and transformation of the company and may even create extra competitive advantages. In other cases, the new comers may carry with them strong entrepreneur spirit and thus boost colleague morale in the workplace. However, while there are various sorts of benefits that new comers may bring about, few of those benefits could be count on and thus practically speaking, only participating in and maintaining daily business of the host company is the realistic expectation for entry-level candidates.

For jobs as simple as maintaining daily business, there is a requirement of skills, and thus recruiters will expect certain level of skills from young people. Once we have finished discussing the benefits of recruiting new entry-level candidates, we need to discuss about what costs that new recruitments will incur.

Are there any costs? Sure, apparently.

The most obviously cost incurred to the firm is the salary and compensation package that the new employees earn, and training costs that the firm pays to help those new comers develop skills may also become part of total cost. However, for an entry-level employee the compensation package is generally small, and companies will certainly not pay too much compared with that new candidate's contribution. What's more, costs such as compensation package are tangible and measurable, which are also controllable and predictable, and thus they won't bring much trouble to companies. In other cases, companies might not be so relieved, and there is one case that an entry-level employee may bring problems to the employer and possibly induce tremendous losses.

As an old saying goes, *the rotten apple injures its neighbors*. In any organization, the irresponsibility exhibited by one member will endanger the well-being of other members. One potential cost for the firm's hiring new staffs is the unfavorable impact that the new employees might have over the corporate culture, or the atmosphere of firm. For instance, for a company that highlights teamwork and share-spirit, it is better not to recruit a new employee who prefers working alone, in which case the efficiency of the whole team might drop. Sheeroy Desai, CEO of recruitment software company GILD, once said that the cost of a bad hire might grow geometrically, which did not only include time and budget of arranging another recruitment, but also the possible change of corporate culture.[59]

Similarly, Christine Porath (2016)[60] introduced in her article a study[61] by Minor and Housman, which analyzes the destructive power of rogue employees based on an empirical study of 60,000 employees coming from 11 companies in 6 industries[i]. The result of their study shows that one rogue employee would ruin the economic benefits created by more than two star-employees. And to be specific, the extra revenues created by a star employee is around $5,000 per year, but the extra cost generated by a rogue employee could be as high as $12,000 each year, and when taking into consideration of other potential costs like the spread of bad practice or lawsuit charges, the destructive power of a rogue employee would be even higher. In fact, in the case of the former paragraph, Sheeroy Desai has also related data showing that the average cost of recruitment failure is 5 times larger than the annual salary of recruited employee.

Let's use a simple arithmetical expression to illustrate this idea. Suppose there are 9 members in a team, with the average productivity of each member being 0.9, and the performance figure of the whole team is thus $(0.9+0.1) * 9$, with the added 0.1 to the productivity of each employee is due to the positive teamwork effect created by collaboration among team members. Now an entry-level new member joins this team and his productivity is 0.6. When the new member could not fit in the work environment that other members have got used to and reduces positive synergy among team members, the performance figure of the whole team now becomes $(0.9-0.1)*9+(0.6-0.1)$, where -0.1 represents the reduced efficiency to each member's productivity led by the adverse influence of the new employee. Under this situation, the performance of the whole team is much worse than the original one, since the positive synergy inside the team has been replaced by a negative one.

Warren Buffett said, "Somebody once said that in looking for people to hire, you look for three qualities: integrity, intelligence, and energy. And

---

[i] Those industries include telecommunication, customer service, financial service, health care, insurance and retailing

if you don't have the first, the other two will kill you. You think about it; it's true. If you hire somebody without integrity, you really want them to be dumb and lazy." When understand these words using the arithmetical expression proposed just now, we know if the influence of new comers to the original organization is negative, employers would suffer a loss, and when this harmful effect grows larger and reaches a level of -0.3, the whole efficiency of the team becomes 5.7[i], which is certainly unacceptable for the firm.

For young people, even if they do not intend to, some of their behaviors release signals that would make employers uncomfortable and employers have every reason to get worried. For example, as has been mentioned before, some young job seekers are considered by employers as unemployable, since they're not aware of the negative consequences of their actions and care little about other things besides what they want. But I would never state that some youths are mean to be such bad, instead, I would prefer saying that these youths are just not fully aware of their responsibility to the business environment and do not understand their role when they are at work—which is certainly different from home environment as well as school environment. I am confident that if young people have prepared well, they will understand their role and responsibility as employees but now, how should we summarize the status that many youths have been described by employers as unemployable?

I would use the word "X-factor" to describe young people's problem in this aspect, which I will provide my reasons in the next section. Up to now, it is an analysis from the cost aspect, and since tangible costs such as compensation packages and training costs are relatively small and less of a concern than the possibility of a bad hire, and thus I would state that the consideration of cost of recruiting entry-level candidates from the perspective of recruiters becomes an issue of X-factor of job applicants.

When we conclude the illustration of benefits and costs analysis, we would further find that all our discussions actually are related to two aspects of job seekers—the unemployed youth: skill-related issue and X-factor. Skill-related issues help recruiters to understand whether the youth could contribute to the daily operation of the firm, which constitutes a main part of benefits, and X-factor helps recruiters to predict whether they would make a bad hire, which is a major concern from cost aspect. Now, the benefits and costs analysis could be transformed into the analysis of skill-related issue and X-factor related

---

[i] $(0.9-0.3)*9+(0.6-0.3)$

issue. Note that these two issues are relatively independent, but in fact, as Torres (2015) has stated in her article[62] the finding of Minor and Housman, that there is likely a trade-off between productivity and toxic character at work, there may also exist trade-off between skill-related issues and X-factor related issues.

4.4 The X-factor

In the former section, I have used "X-factor" to reflect the concern of cost of new recruitment for a company, which indicates the worry of employers that their newly hired employees may become "toxic" workers in the future. When we look at the description "X-factor", it seems that this word could mean anything and thus tells us nothing, which as a result, is inappropriate to be used here.

In fact, when I just started to write this chapter, I have never thought of using "X-factor" to represent the concern about cost of recruitment, instead I have tried to use descriptions like "moral character" "well-being" "habit" or "socialization" to fill in the position where belongs to "X-factor" now. And Torres (2015) has also related in her article[63] the research conducted by Minor and Housman and stated that characters and personal traits like overconfident, self-centered, productive and rule-following may be some good predictive indicators of toxic workers. However, none of these words could satisfy me. There always exist doubts, and none of them could reassure me and make me feel comfortable as what "X-factor" does.

The key concern for me is that none of those words except for "X-factor" could explicitly describe the original concern, which is the worry of employers that their new employees might become "toxic workers" and thus want to evaluate something about their applicants—the original concern is to use a word to generalize this "something". What's more, as these words could not answer the original concern, they bring about new questions and problems. For example, I have tried to use "socialization" and "socialization-related issue" to fill in the position of "X-factor", and the definition of socialization from Merriam-Webster dictionary is as follows: the process by which a human being beginning at infancy acquires the habits, beliefs, and accumulated knowledge of society through education and training for adult status[64]. My justification for using "socialization" here was that to work is essentially to cope with different people in the social environment, and the reason why some youths behave improperly in work environment, such as being late for work frequently or keeping complaining about their work conditions, or make recruiters during the interview worry that they might have such behaviors after being hired, is that these youths are not familiar with work environment, not realizing expectations about their conducts from their colleagues and not realizing their responsibilities towards employers. And I once think this reflects potential problems concerning teamwork as adults, which thus might be summarized used the word "socialization".

However, my doubt about using "socialization" has persisted until I replace it with another word. This is because as I have mentioned just now that the word "socialization" cannot meet my expectation of answering the original concern, which is not explicit and would create too much puzzles. For example, if socialization-related issue reflects the possibility of new hires being toxic workers, does it mean a shy candidate who prefers work alone has a higher risk of being toxic than a candidate who is used to public speaking? Certainly not, and apparently, socialization is not a proper word to be used here and so are other alternatives.

In fact, there is no such one description that relates to whether one candidate would become a toxic worker, since it is such a broad topic and even if there is one, to which degree recruiters could follow and make the right decision still remains obscure. Besides, in a recent article[65], Chamorro-Premuzic (2017) introduced 11 "dark side" traits of working people that were proposed by Robert and Hogan, and based on the finding of his company, Hogan Development Survey (HDS), he states that most people show at least 3 out of 11 dark-side traits. Noticed that his statement is based on a data sample consisting of millions of working people, which is large enough to make the judgement that all most all people share some similarities with toxic workers. Does this mean that most people should not be hired? Of course not, especially when we realize that Chamorro-Premuzic's conclusion is based on the data of working people, who're currently being employed.

As a result, it is difficult to use just one or two words to generalize the worry of employers to make a bad hire during recruitment. And, this is where the description "X-factor" helps.

The word chosen should help employers to assess their worry about making a bad hire, and X-factor" could remind employers about this worry since it tells nothing and thus bring about a feeling of uncertainty, which would trigger unease. It is said that business people hate surprise, which is largely because the feeling of uncertainty brought about by surprise would give them a feeling of losing order and control. When faced with candidates' improper behavior such as being late, employers would worry that this might be a sign of potential toxic workers. They are not sure about this judgment, but the feeling of uncertainty is real, and so is the doubt, and the expression of "X-factor" could reflect such kinds of concern and worry of employers: they have the feeling of unease and cannot help but doubt about one candidate, even though they may not know exactly what's wrong with the candidate or where the problem is.

The term "fair use" would be a good example for us to better understand the role of X-factor here. "Fair use" is well-known among people in the publishing industry, whether they are writers, agencies, or publishers. However, there isn't a clear definition of fair use and it remains obscure about to which degree it would be considered as fair use. Even if it is vague, due to its popularity and significance, no one could neglect its existence and such concern, otherwise they are risking their reputation and career.

My expectation about X-factor is similar to that of fair use, that both of them remind people of certain important issues, yet people cannot grasp the whole stuff even if they understand these terms, simply because they are obscure. The concern about fair use between writers and copyright owners are similar to the concern about X-factor between job seekers and recruiters. Some copyright owners, especially those big publishers, will make it clear about their own policies about fair use, but in most cases, writers may have to contact copyright owners to seek written permissions for using a very small part of copyright materials. This is the same for jobs seekers, that they may have to figure out what "X-factor" means for different companies.

And thus, what has made the expression "X-factor" especially helpful is that it could not only reflect employers' concerns, but also indicate young people what they should do before applying for employment: they need to take the initiative to explore and find out what kinds of employees that recruiters need and expect. Just like employers, young people cannot get any information from the expression of "X-factor", but they know there is one such thing for recruitment, and thus they should strive to discover what "X-factor" means for the specific company that they are applying for. Just as fair use policies, X-factor concerns vary among companies, and in some cases, the same thing may even affect the concern about X-factor conversely. For example, among the 11 "dark side" traits of working people proposed by Robert and Hogan, the character of cautious might be good for some firms and be bad for some other firms.

The expression "X-factor" would help clarify questions relating to labor supply and labor demand, which has made it suited to be used in my framework. On one hand, it indicates the worry of recruiters that their job applicants might be toxic workers, and they hope to avoid such uncertainty during their recruitment; and on the other hand, it reminds young people that they should take the initiative, whether through internship experience, training programs or just searching relevant information on the Internet, to explore and find out what employers need and how should they behave to meet those needs.

Here about the improper behavior of young people, "X-factor" indicates the possibility of being a toxic worker, and I have a sound reason concerning why it is inappropriate to use "toxic-related issue" in my framework.

Some youths have improper behaviors, which may cause harm to companies, and for employers, they have every reason to worry about the possibility of these young people becoming toxic workers, since they are not willing to bear the burden of recruiting even one toxic worker. But for us to understand young people and their unemployment, we cannot take their improper behaviors as a sign of being toxic workers, since there are so many of young people, and to use "toxic" to describe large amount of youths is not only unfair but also unreasonable.

In reality, people would prepare for interviews and generally speaking, they would tend to hide the real them to cater the expectations of recruiters. Remember in classes concerning interview preparation, instructors have reminded the audience to do something and avoid doing something else? The case that job seekers might disguise themselves has complicated the description and there are at least two types of improper behaviors in work place: one is intended to and the other is not intended to. For the large number of unemployed young people, I will not state that they are intended to perform poorly, which is described by employers as a sign of being unemployable, instead, I prefer to say that they are just not fully aware of the effect of their behaviors towards their companies.

Our world is not perfect, and whether applicants will trigger the worry of employers relates to how well these applicants know and behave as is expected by employers, which might have no direct link with how competent these applicants really are. The expression "X-factor" informs young people that they need to find out what employers need and perform accordingly, and only so would they pass recruitment and get a job.

4.5 Long-term concern of recruitment

According to the recruitment formula, the decision of recruitment is based on one thing: benefit is believed to be larger than the relevant cost, and this inequation is expected to hold in the long-term. Now we have to ask, what will determine that whether this inequation will hold or not in the future? For a young person who has the right set of skills and behaves well in work place, it is reasonable to believe that he will keep making progress during his stay in the company and thus this inequation will always hold. Then why would employers still worry about whether this inequation will hold in the long-term?

For companies, they recruit entry-level employees or fresh graduates not only for the purpose of fulfilling current needs of their businesses, but also hope to cultivate future leaders, whether to become stars of certain business lines or to become managers of certain departments. From the perspective of employers, they hope a suited employee could stay long in the company, especially when these candidates have fulfilled the first requirement: they create much more benefits than costs to the firm.

But from the perspective of employees, to work for one company for their lifetime may not be the best choice, and to change jobs is in fact quite common nowadays. This is especially true for young people, who are eager to experience more and explore more about their potentials. When a newly enrolled employee resigns and works for another company, benefits he brings to the former company ends and if so, costs that the former company has spent to train him would not get compensated. Since changing jobs is such a common phenomenon in most job markets, employers have to take it into consideration when they recruit new employees.

What factors might influence the length of newly recruited employees' staying period in a company? And are there any factors that could help employers to predict this sort of issue?

Many factors would lead to one's decision of resigning, such as there is another company that offers him a better salary package, better working conditions, better career prospect or something else. While these factors do matter much, they happen in the unforeseeable future, or otherwise a reasonable person won't turn down these jobs and choose a suboptimum one. Recruiters of the original companies don't know whether there will there be another company that is extremely interested in one employee that they've decided to hire, and thus these factors should not be taken into consideration during recruitment process.

However, there is certainly one thing that a recruiter hopes to know, which is whether the candidate has sincere interest in his company. Many tools and methods have been developed to help recruiters to assess the interest of job seekers, and I won't spend time on this aspect. My question is that does it really matter that whether candidates have sincere interest[i] in the firm that they are applying for?

Yes, it does. And this is because having interest or not relates to how hardworking young people would be on their jobs. When they first step into job market, they will take on some basic responsibilities, which are generally full of easy tasks. If candidates do not have sincere interest in the job, they will easily get tired and bored, which would make them become less efficient. More importantly, interest matters in predicting one's stay in one company. If a person has strong interest in one company, or the business that the company is engaged in, he will typically stay longer in the company compared to those who are not so interested in. And this is why motivation is a very important thing that recruiters are eager to know about their candidates: what's your motivation of applying our firms?

In reality, people apply for jobs in a company with many different motivations. One case is that they are really interested in the company, and they submit their application. In another case, candidates do not take seriously about their application, but just want to have someone to pay them salaries. In this second case, candidates apply for positions in some companies just for the purpose of a temporary stay, whether due to their lack of competencies for their ideal companies or due to a lack of job opportunities during economic downturn, which means they have a high possibility of leaving once external factors change. Besides these two cases, there are also people who have no ideas about their career paths, and they just do what is best for them at that time they enter job market. They will apply for companies within their competencies that provide best compensation, and this is the optimal choice for a rational person.

Faced with various motivations of applicants, recruiters' reactions are different. For those candidates who have sincere interest in the firm, recruiters will prefer to accept their applications first. And for those who do not show such interest about the firm, they are expected by recruiters to possess a higher level of skills and to be more competent, or otherwise their applications will be turned down for their uncertain length of period staying in the firm. When candidates are expected to serve the firm only for a short period of time, employers are typically

---

[i] At least make recruiters believe that they are interested in the firm

The Recruitment Formula

not willing to provide resources in training them or helping them develop skills, since when these people resign, the more companies have invested, the more they loss. But for those who are really interested in the firm, who are thus expected to work longer for the firm, employers are more willing to allocate resources to cultivate them and to invest in them, even if the competencies of these people may not be as good as that of others.

As a result, the long-term concern during recruitment actually matters with one thing: candidates' interest. And the expected holding of the inequation [i] in the long run is now converted to one issue: interested-related issue.

Now we have finished the construction of the extended illustration of recruitment formula, which summarizes aspects that recruiters would care about during recruitment. We exhibit this extended illustration of the Recruitment Formula in figure 4.2:

Benefits > Costs?		Hold in long-term?
Skill-related issue	X-factor	Interest-related issue

Figure 4.2 An extended illustration of the Recruitment Formula

4.6 Formula implementation: understanding more facts about labor-supply (1)

In the last section, we have obtained the framework to be used to determine whether young people should also be responsible for their unemployment, and now, what we need to do is to use this framework to analyze more facts from youth labor market and reach a conclusion.

Facts to be analyzed here are mainly derived from the two global surveys conducted by McKinsey Center for Government. Obvious, the way that survey results presented in their reports is highly related to the logic of their study, which is to connect education with employment, and thus, I will present results of their surveys here in my book in a different order, which follows my logic. And also, I will only use data rather than texts

---

[i] Benefits of having an employee are larger than the relevant costs

of their reports, since their data provide more facts on youth unemployment issue. In short, my task here is to dissociate fundamental facts from their presentation of surveys and interpret the implication of these fundamental facts under my framework.

Before we start, let's have a quick review of McKinsey's second cross-border survey of youth unemployment, results of which they present in another report on youth unemployment, *Education to Employment: Getting Europe's Youth into Work*[66]. This second survey focuses on the situation of Europe, including responds from 5,000 young people, 2,400 employers and 800 education providers and the corresponding report covers eight countries: France, Germany, Greece, Italy, Portugal, Spain, Sweden and the Unites Kingdom. According to the appendices of this report, more than 70% of youth unemployment in the European Union happens in these eight countries.

Noticing that Eastern Europe countries such as Poland is not included in their second survey, the rationality of which has been introduced in their report, that "We did not include countries from Eastern Europe, whose history and economic dynamics are distinctive." This explanation let us know that their survey of youth unemployment and the methodology used to solve this problem must have something to do with factors as history and economic dynamics, and this further differentiates my analysis from theirs—even though some of my conclusions are obtained based on their data. As readers will find later in this book, my analysis develops from the perspective of human growth, which thus neglects differences in history, culture and economic dynamics among different countries.

In this part, the findings of MCG will be analyzed along with fragmentary pieces of information I obtained from other sources. Remember that the formula I have proposed contains two aspects—benefits and costs, which is further extended to three components: skill-related issue, X-factor and interest-related issue. Now let's begin with the first component, skill-related issue.

Skill-related issue concerns job applicants' competences to accomplish daily business of firms. Do young people meet this requirement?

One question in MCG's surveys asked respondents their opinions concerning the readiness of fresh graduates for employment, and none of the three kinds of stakeholders fully believe that these graduates are adequately prepared when they step into job market, with the percentage of respondents who believe the youth are adequately prepared on average is 42%, 45% and 72% respectively for employers, youth and education providers.

	Employers	The Youth	Education Providers
Countries of the world	42%	45%	72%
Countries from EU	35%	38%	74%

Table 4.1 Percentages of respondents that agree young people have well prepared

Source: McKinsey Center for Government[67,68]

Categories	Industries	Portions
Industries where more than half companies believe young people are well prepared	Education	54%
	Financial intermediation	52%
	Health and social work	51%
Industries where less than half companies believe young people are well prepared	Other	43%
	Manufacturing	42%
	Construction	41%
	Transport, storage, and communications	41%
	Real estate, renting, and business activities	38%
	Wholesale and retail trade	38%
	Agriculture, hunting, forestry, and fishing	37%
	Hotels and restaurants	35%

Table 4.2 Industry difference concerning the preparedness of young people

Source: McKinsey Center for Government[69]

When focusing on Europe, the situation is worse, with only 35% employer, 38% youth and 74% education providers believing that young people are adequately prepared when they step into job market. Furthermore, when group global employers by sectors, except for three

The Recruitment Formula

sectors (education, financial intermediation and health & social work), less than half of respondents from other sectors believe that their entry-level new-hired employees are well prepared[i]. Data is shown in table 4.1 and table 4.2.

From data above, we know that young people should also be responsible for their unemployment, since they are not believed by employers to prepare well for employment. Besides, more questions concerning skills have been proposed in MCG's surveys.

According to MCG, nearly 39% employers state that a lack of skills is a common reason for the existing of unfilled entry-level job positions and 36% employers report that "a lack of skills caused 'significant problems in terms of cost, quality and time' or worse". This is largely the same result when focus on Europe, and on average 33% employers believes a lack of skills affects their business adversely. The word "skill" in MCG's statement that "a lack of skills caused 'significant problems in terms of cost, quality and time' or worse" is almost the same as the "skill" in my description that "skill-related issue", and thus I say that skill-related issue matters in young people's unemployment and thus is one cause for youth unemployment crisis.

I use "almost the same" to describe the relationship between "skill" appears in MCG's report and the one appears in my book, and this is because the "skill" used in MCG's report is actually a broader concept, which will not only help us determine whether or not skill-related issue matters in youth unemployment problem, but also help us figure out whether X-factor also matters for youth unemployment.

In both of MCG's two surveys, there is a question asking employers' opinions about how important some skills are for entry-level employees and how competent their entry-level candidates are. An illustration of the result of this question is shown in figure 4.3, and let's focus on one kind of skill: work ethic. As we can see, work ethic ranks as the most important skill for entry-level employees and the gap between its importance and the competence of youth is also one of the largest, and this is generally the same for all European countries.

---

[i] I am really excited that McKinsey has asked this question in the survey, since result of this question helps to justify one key judgment that will be presented later in this book: whether young people should also be responsible for their unemployment

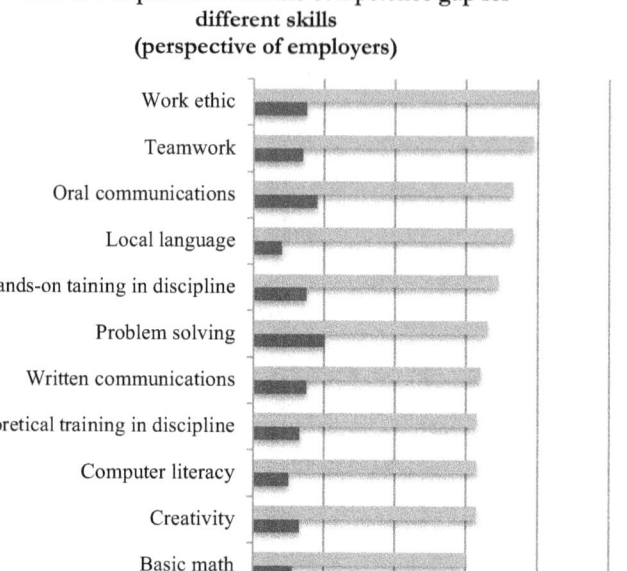

Figure 4.3 Relative importance and the competence gap for different skills

Source: McKinsey Center for Government[70]

How should we understand the "work ethic" presented here?

Apparently, work ethic doesn't equal to ethic or moral character, and as has been discussed in section 4.3, whether or not a person is competent for a specific job has no direct link with his moral trait. By adding a word "work" before "ethic", the term must have something to do with workplace. Some people may consider that not willing to work from the bottom as a sign of lacking work ethic, and in some cultures, to be on time for work would indicate work ethic.

If we hold an assumption that young people are not intended to behave bad, but genuinely believe the rationality of their behaviors, then young people's appearance of lacking work ethic, is not a question of moral character, but a question of cognition. On one hand, many youths do not recognize the importance of basic tasks and are unwilling to start from the bottom; on that other hand, they do not fully realize the expectations of others, especially the expectations that employers hold about them in workplace.

I would conclude that this relates to X-factor. Young people do not show strong work ethic which reminds employers of something they dislike, such as toxic workers or bad hires. This would rouse the feeling of unease and uncertainty, just as the meaning that X-factor represents. Thus, the appearance of lacking work ethic believed by employers actually matches our discussion of X-factor, and this has prevented many youths from getting employment and has left plenty of entry-level job vacancies.

The conclusion is that X-factor also plays a role in understanding the existing of entry-level job vacancies, just as skill-related issue does.

4.7 Formula implementation: understanding more facts about labor-supply (2)

In the former section, we have identified the involvement of skill-related issue and X-factor in the occurring of youth unemployment problem, and in this section, I will try to figure out whether interest-related issue also matters.

There is no data in MCG's reports that could help us determine directly whether interest-related issue matters in youth unemployment, but we could deduce and reach a conclusion based on results of their surveys. Even if we don't know exactly whether young people have sincere interest for companies that they are applying for, we do know what people look like when they have sincere interest for something.

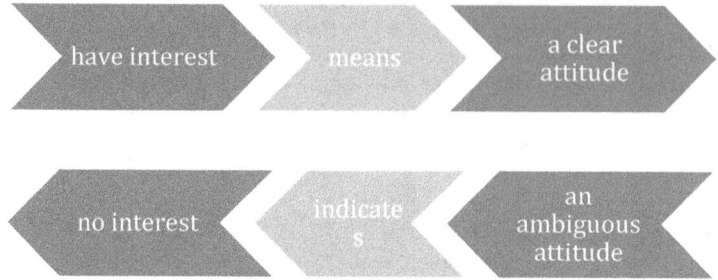

Figure 4.4 The relationship between attitude and interest

Consider a question like this: what kind of a person would he become if he knows his interest about certain jobs? When one person has interest for certain kind of jobs, he won't puzzle over questions like what kind of jobs he likes or has no idea about his interest. If so, the question of whether young people have sincere interest for certain positions could be deduced based on an examination about whether young people have a clear attitude: to possess a clear attitude to something is a sign of interest.

Now we need to ask, do young people have a clear attitude? If they do not exhibit a kind of clear attitude to their employment, we know that they haven't realized their own interest, not to mention their interests for jobs that they are applying for.

MCG's two reports are organized following the idea of better education leading to proper employment, and there are three stages in this logic line, which could be classified as pre-education, education and post-education (entering job market to seek employment). Even if we do not possess data telling us the situation of young people at the third stage—post-education, we could deduce and reach a conclusion about this issue by observing their performance in the former two stages: stage of pre-education and stage of education. And luckily, we do find data in MCG's surveys showing us the situation of young people at the first two stages.

According to MCG's reports, less than half young people have enough knowledge about the subjects that they've chosen to learn, which provides a sign that before education, many youths do not have a clear idea about their future careers—when they don't know exactly which subjects to learn, they would definitely have no idea about employment. At the same time, also according to MCG's reports, less than one third of young people think they have obtained sufficient information and career advice during their secondary education. This tells us that concerning the knowledge of their desired jobs, young people do not improve much during their education period.

When they do not possess a clear attitude towards their future employment at pre-education stage and do not improve much on this aspect during their stay at school, we could then state that many youths do not form a clear attitude towards jobs that are suitable for them, which, as is illustrated in figure 4.4, also means that they do not have sincere interest for jobs that they are applying for. The logic here is shown in table 4.3, in which stage-3 is the time period that we are care about.

Stage-1: Pre-education stage	Stage 2: Education stage	Stage 3: Post-education stage
No sincere interest	Make little progress	No sincere interest

Table 4.3 Young people's interest towards jobs

Now we know that young people have also problems concerning interest-related issue, and this makes it more difficult for them to get employment.

In fact, interest-related issue will affect young people's employment more or less, since during recruitment, recruiters would make a tradeoff between candidates' skills and their interest for the firm, and the more skilled a candidate is, the less interested that recruiters would demand. The opposite is true, that the more interested a candidate is in a firm, the less skilled he would need to pass recruitment.

There is a sort of negative correlation existing between skills required and level of interest required, which is shown in figure 4.5. Noticed that the line isn't a straight line but is a hyperbola, since for a candidate, the skills he possesses or the interest he has for the firm cannot be too little, and once his competences reach a certain low level, he would not be able to pass the interview unless he exhibits extremely strong interest for the firm. This is the same for a candidate who shows a low level of interest for the firm that he is applying for.

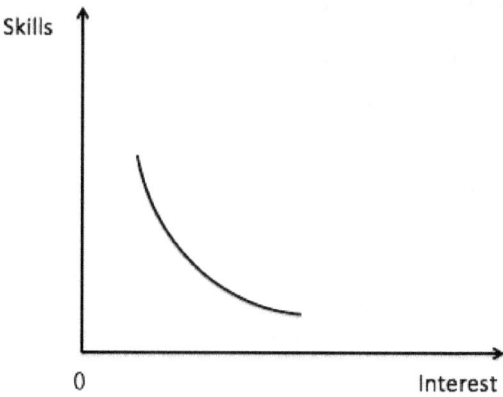

Figure 4.5 Adverse relationship exists between skills required and interest required

From analysis in the former section, we know that many youths lack required skills and do not exhibit strong work ethic, which makes it less likely that they would fulfill the requirement on interest, since when their skills are not good enough, the expected level of interest moves higher. Traditionally, young people keep shifting positions in different firms to explore their own interest, after which they will find their suitable jobs. This means when they step out of school and seek employment, young people typically have only a little knowledge about themselves and about job market, and if so, they could hardly have any sincere interest for any job position or any company.

Based on the discussion of section 4.5 and 4.6, the Recruitment Formula has helped us to understand the strange phenomenon that there is large amount of youths who do not have jobs and meantime, there are many entry-level job vacancies. Thus, we conclude that young people should also be responsible for this youth unemployment crisis, or in other words, young people's unemployment is their own problem, not that of others.

Up to now, we have made some progress: we find young people should also be responsible for their unemployment, since they are not believed by employers to be competent enough for employment. This helps but is not the end of our analysis, since we have to find out why young people do not meet the expectation of employers.

The Recruitment Formula

5. YOUTH UNEMPLOYMENT AND WEALTH INEQUALITY

5.1 A further exploration of reasons behind youth unemployment

Based on discussions in chapter 4, we conclude that young people should also be responsible for their unemployment, since they fail to meet expectations of employers. But this is not the end of our analysis, since we haven't reached a point based on which we could propose plans to solve youth unemployment problem.

For example, we would not simply state that we should help young people build skills or make them be aware of the discipline in workplace, since we still don't know why these youths fail to meet the expectation of employers and just acknowledging their failure like this is not a proper start for proposing solutions. And thus, let's continue our analysis based on the perspective of labor-supply and, yes, following the one-stakeholder approach.

		Care a lot about edu & career options	Care a little about edu & career options
High school only		Too poor (43%): not afford to	Too cool (57%): not interested in
With post-secondary education	Well informed	Well positioned (20%): focused & prepared	Not identified
	Moderately informed	Driven (18%): motivated	Disheartened (17%): Known enough
	Ill-informed	Struggling (26%): Eager for more information	Disengaged (18%): Don't care about information

Table 5.1 Young people's interest towards jobs

Source: McKinsey Center for Government[71]

Let's begin with one case that I pick up from MCG's reports. In report *Education to Employment: Designing A System that Works*, the authors once divide young people into two groups, one with post-secondary education experience and the other with only high school education experience. As shown in table 5.1, these young people are further divided into seven segments, with the group with only high school education experience consisting of two segments: the first one is described as "too poor to afford higher education", and the second one to be "'too cool' to receive higher education", which means youths in this category are not "interested" in pursuing post-secondary education[72].

The idea of being too cool to pursue further study does sound cool, but is this a reasonable and reliable answer?

No, at least not for me. This feeling is like a disciplined and punctual person coming late for work, with an explanation that he oversleeps: you know this is not the truth and you would rather believe that he helped somebody on his way to work and thus got delayed. The feeling here is that the answer given is not reliable and you know there is something else behind it, the real reason. The reply of "too cool to go on study" gives me the same feeling, that it is not a trustworthy answer.

Are there any implicit subtexts in the statement of "too cool to study"?

In both of MCG's two reports on youth unemployment, there are data obtained from reports of OECD, which tell us that there is a positive net present value (NPV) of tertiary education from a life-long perspective[73], a result that is the same for both males and females[74]. Under this acknowledgement, and with the assumption that those who have replied too cool to study could afford the cost of further education, would a rational person go on pursuing tertiary education? The answer would most likely to be yes.

If those young people who express "too cool" to receive higher level of education realize the positive value of tertiary education, would they still be cool about their decision to terminate their study? If they could afford further education, would they simply change their minds and go to college? What if these young people's reply of "too cool" happens not for their unwillingness of study, but for their inability to afford further study? And if that the answer of being "too cool to study" is indeed a result of those young people's choice, rather than their poverty, we would prefer to understand the group of young people who are too cool to study as not possessing the right information about the positive value of tertiary education—as we can see from table 5.1, young people in this segment only care a little about educational and career options, which means it is highly likely that they are short of proper information.

When we understand the two segments of young people in the group that did not attend post-secondary education, these two segments could be actually converted from "too poor to study" and "too cool to study", to "too poor to study" and "too ill-informed to study". In fact, as is revealed in MCG's reports[i], cost remains as the most important cause underlying young people's not pursuing post-secondary education, and information also plays a key role. Since the segment of too cool to study for many young people could be further understood as a lack of adequate information and then, the lack of tertiary education could be understood from the aspect of wealth and the aspect of information.

Remember in section 2.6, I have proposed data showing a general tendency that as education level rises, youth unemployment rate falls, and in this section, we would know that those with only high school experience have higher youth unemployment rate and suffer more from youth unemployment problem. As a result, through their impacts on

---

[i] Throughout my book, "McKinsey's (first) report" or "MCG's (first) report" refers to Education to Employment: Designing a system that works issued by McKinsey Center for Government in Dec 2012 and "McKinsey's second report" or "MCG's second report" refers to Education to Employment: Getting Europe's Youth into Work issued by McKinsey Center for Government in Jan 2014. Both of these two reports are available from the website of McKinsey

level of education, wealth and information contribute to the explanation of occurring of youth unemployment problem: many youths suffer from unemployment because they do not possess a higher level of degree, which is further because they are short of wealth and information.

Based on the illustration of relationship between level of education and youth unemployment rate, we find the roles of wealth and information behind youth unemployment problem. Now we can't help wondering, what is exactly the role of wealth and information in the occurring of youth unemployment crisis? This is a question we are eager to know, and I will figure this out with the help of the Recruitment Formula that I have proposed in chapter 4.

5.2 Wealth matters

Could things related to wealth help us understand the existing of youth unemployment problem? To answer this question, let's focus our attention on "recruitment" for the second time and to analyze following the extended framework of Recruitment Formula. Remember that Recruitment Formula summarizes the principle that recruiters follow to make decisions about whether to hire one candidate, which could be extended into three aspects: skill-related issue, X-factor and interest-related issue.

Firstly, the relationship between wealth and skill-related issue, or relationship between wealth and the formation of skills.

Education plays an important role in young people's building of skills and as is revealed in MCG's survey, cost remains as the most important barrier that stops young people from attending university or finishing their study there. Cost relates to money, which is also known as wealth.

Besides building skills through education, young people could also build their skills through participating in training programs. However, the operation of these training programs requires budget and except for limited opportunities provided by companies with the purpose of recruiting potential employees or those provided by governmental agencies for the benefit of society, young people have to pay for their taking part in these training programs or workshops, which requires wealth.

Skills would not be developed by simply sitting on the couch at home, and they could only be strengthened by keep practicing. If there is no place for young people to develop and practice their skills, their skills won't grow: this is where wealth helps, since wealthy people could pay for additional training programs or other workshops. And, in fact, child labor regulations have reinforced the importance of wealth on the building of skills—for those who enter job market at a young age, they may not have the chance to develop skills for their lack of wealth. As is required by law, children too young cannot be hired to work, and due to their lack of wealth, many children cannot afford other training programs or workshops that would help them build skills. As a result, when they enter job market to seek employment at a young age that is just old enough to work legally, they have little work experience and are not skilled, and this makes them less likely to get proper employment.

As a result, level of wealth affects the formation of skills.

Secondly, the relationship between wealth and the concern of X-factor.

X-factor reflects employers' concern that they may make a bad hire, or recruit toxic workers, and if employers notice such a concern for one candidate, generally there would be two cases: one case is that the candidate is actually not a "toxic worker", but his performance makes him look like a "toxic worker"; and the other case is that the candidate does have the potential to become "toxic workers" from the standpoint of employers.

For the first case, that the candidate makes mistakes which gets himself look like a "toxic worker". This case occurs largely because the candidate doesn't understand the needs of the company that he is applying for. When candidates have no idea about what kinds of employees one specific company likes, there is a large possibility that they would make mistakes during recruitment. And wealth helps in this aspect. For example, candidates could seek the advice of fee-paid professionals to help them obtain such information or take part in some mock interviews to prepare for the formal one. When they are aware of what types of employees the target company doesn't like, they will avoid behaviors that might make recruiters worry and arouse their alertness.

And for the second case, that the candidate is indeed a potential "toxic worker" from the standpoint of employers, wealth also matters. For example, social activities and traveling could help a person become more opened, but all these activities need the support of wealth, to cover transportation expenses, hotel bills, and restaurant charges. And in fact, education could also help young people become more socialized but just as has been mentioned, cost, and thus wealth, gets in the way towards education. And, all these have demonstrated the relationship between wealth and the concern of X-factor.

Thirdly, the aspect of interest-related issue.

The formation of interest for certain types of jobs consisting of an understanding of oneself and an understanding of job market. With adequate wealth, young people could better explore and establish their own interest, since they have more opportunities to follow their interests and do the sort of things they'd like to do. For example, a child may finally find his sincere interest in painting after taking part in training courses of many different subjects, such as sports, writing, music or painting.

Besides taking part in activities—which there is certainly a need of wealth, taking some standardized psychological tests, such as MBTI or DISC test, is also a common way to understand oneself better. But most of these tests are provided not for free, and one has to make a payment each time of taking test, the charge of which may be too costly for some youths. Even if there are similar and simplified tests provided for free, the effectiveness of those simplified tests many be reduced and thus prevent the test-takers from knowing themselves better. The conclusion is that, wealth matters in interest-related issue too.

Up to now, I have focused on the extended version of Recruitment Formula to understand the role of wealth, but in reality, the role of wealth could be found everywhere. For example, young people's not willing to take up low-paid jobs. While the importance of work experience has been stressed by recruiters, and to take up low-paid jobs during economy downturn is a reasonable choice for many youths, for those who have been suffering from poverty during their growing up, their tolerance with low-paid jobs tend to be much lower than those who have no experience of poverty. This is because large amount of wealth is required to keep a certain standard of living, and if the original level of accumulated wealth is relatively small, there will be a need of income from employment. This has made it less likely for young people to accept low-paid jobs, and as a result, young people's tendency to turn down low-paid jobs has something to do with their wealth status too.

Now we know that wealth plays a key role in understanding the existence of youth unemployment problem.

5.3 Information matters

Does Information also matter in the occurring of youth unemployment problem? Let's figure it out in this section.
Remember in table 5.1, for those who are classified as ill-informed or moderately informed, there are certain percentage of youth who "care a little" about educational and career options, but for those who are well informed, nearly all of them "care a lot" about these options, which means there is no such a "sizable and distinct segment" that who are well informed yet care little about education and career options.

According to the result of MCG's second report[75], only youths in the high achiever segment could find suitable employment quickly and at the same time, be satisfied with their employment. And generally, young people in this segment have more knowledge on labor market issues, such as "which discipline has more job opportunities", "which industries have high wages" and "which educational providers have good job-placement rates". The high achievers on employment have more information on job market, does this happen by chance?

Definitely not. Let's take a case for example: employers sometimes show their desirability for candidates with volunteer experience, but from the perspective of young people, would they like to do volunteer work? And if they possess enough information, would their attitude towards volunteer positions change?

For young people who know little about job market, volunteer experience is perhaps not attractive for them. However, if they know recruiters' opinions about volunteer work, and more specifically, if they realize that recruiters' expectations about skills of young people are more likely general ones such as language skills or people skills, and realize that these skills could actually be developed through their experience of volunteer work, would they become more willing and engaged to volunteer work? The answer would largely be yes.

Proper information would help people make better choices and concerning employment, information on job market enables young people to have a long-term view about causal relationships existing in job market, which help them to prepare accordingly.

In order to have an intuitive view about the role of information, let's consider a question like this: for today's children, who are still young to enter job market seeking employment, would their career prospects be better the those who are seeking employment now[i]? If they have realized the difficulty of seeking employment and prepare accordingly, such as taking part in some volunteer activities, they will suffer less from unemployment, simply because employers are more willing to recruit them. This is the role of information, enabling people to prepare for the future and making better choices from the perspective of future.

Now, let's come back to our extended version of Recruitment Formula to understand the importance of information in the occurring of youth unemployment problem.

Firstly, skill-related issue.

Besides education, another factor that is commonly discussed in skill aspect is a lack of work experience, which could be considered as a lack of internship experience before entering job market to seek full-time jobs.

Many youths do not realize the importance of internship until they are trying to get a full-time position, and for many other youths, they are not interested in internship positions, especially for those they are "over-qualified" to work for. Most youths expect to have decent jobs and hope to play an important role in the business world. But from the standpoint of employers, basic skills would still be expected for their candidates, and these skills could be developed through simple work experience. To hire a candidate who has some work experience would be better than those who have no previous work experience, since this would at least save training cost. If young people know the importance of internship and have taken up enough internships, they would less likely get rejected by employers for lacking skills.

Secondly, X-factor related issue.

To be able to get used to different environments and cope well with people, the key point is that one must first know what he should do in certain circumstances. And there are generally two methods to achieve this: one is learning through first-hand experience, which could be accumulated through personal experience; and the other is learning through second-hand experience, which comes from other people, such as reading relevant books or attending workshops.

Information has been important for both of these two methods. To

---

[i] Suppose external factors such as macroeconomic conditions and job market situations remain the same

gain first-hand experience, one must take part in enough activities, and only knowing the importance of accumulating first-hand experience, would young people actively participate in more activities, otherwise they may stay in their comfort zone and not willing to come out. Similarly, the role of information could be easily identified in the second method, since the building of second-hand experience rely on messages from other people, and "messages" here could be considered as a form of information.

When one person knows what employers desire, and in order to dispel the doubt of employers, they will perform accordingly. If so, recruiters would be more likely to think that they would make a good hire instead of a bad one, and the candidate thus has better chance of getting an offer. The thing is, ahead of proper behavior, job seekers must first possess these types of information.

Thirdly, interest-related issue.

Interest-related issue pays attention to the question that whether young people know what types of work that fit their interests and for them to figure this out, there is a need for them to know themselves well and to know different types of job positions well. Both of these would require information, since to know oneself means possessing the information about the characteristics of himself, and to know workplace means possessing the information about the characteristics of different jobs.

All these means, information is closely related to interest-related issue. Now we know, just as wealth, information matters much in understanding the happening of youth unemployment problem.

5.4 Wealth, information and youth unemployment

Ideally, young people enter job market and obtain those jobs that match their interests and abilities. To achieve this, besides the general need of possessing relevant skills, there is also a need of understanding oneself as well as workplace, which includes but not limit to realizing one's strengths and weaknesses, and one's career expectations and the requirements of different jobs. However, this ideal case not be realistic for most people, which means when they enter job market, they have neither adequate knowledge about job market nor essential skills. This might not happen as a result of someone's fault, but do indicate young people's lack of wealth, lack of information, or the lack of both.

Based on former sections, we know that both wealth and information matter in young people's unemployment, and let's review this idea through a brief illustration of education. Before entering job market to seek employment, young people will typically spend some time studying at school, and this experience has a special implication for their employment. Data show that the level of education has a reverse relationship with unemployment rate, and the group of people with post-secondary diplomas have lower level of youth unemployment rate compared with those who have received less education. Many youths do not have the opportunity to attend higher level of education for cost issue, and even if they have attended higher level of education, they may still not be able to benefit much from that experience, and an uninterested discipline to study would greatly discourage them. Why choose an uninterested discipline? A lack of information.

While we know wealth and information matter in young people's employment issue, we should also know that the impact of wealth and the impact of information could not separate from each other but making a difference on young people's employment competencies collectively. Again, let's check this idea through the example of education. It is known to all that even with a university degree (thus little problem with wealth), one may still be unable to find jobs after graduation (for lack of proper information). At the same time, just possessing information is not enough, and we could find such evidences from McKinsey's surveys that concerning the amount of information owned, the group of youth called "persisters" doesn't fall behind too much compared with the group titled "high achievers", and for certain sorts of information, they may possess even more than the high achiever group. However, the achievements of "persisters" in reality do not match with their ambitions for their lack of support, which relates to wealth.

Once realized the role of wealth and information, now we are wondering that to which extend could the lack of wealth and the lack of information explain young people's unemployment?

There is a well-known assumption in economic analysis, which is often called the rational man. While there have emerged many challenges about this assumption, such as behavior finance theories, it is still helpful and insightful to be used in analyzing unemployment issue.

This is because whether or not buying a product or things like that has only limited implication on people, which is further deceased for its limited implication in the future. But this is not the same for employment issue, since employment brings income, which is the basis for keeping a proper living standard. And unemployment now may cause adverse effects on people's future employment prospect, which have made it a real critical issue. According to consumer theory, employment issue thus "has little elasticity": young people do not have much choices other than trying their best to find a job.

Employment is more like a sort of "necessities", which leaves little room for people to decide whether or not seeking employment. As a result, we could apply rational man assumption in our analysis and when we do things like this, and ask if a rational person knows what he should do (have proper information) and could obtain external sources that would help him fulfill his goal (with adequate wealth), would it almost certain that he could get a job? —Generally speaking, yes.

Under this consideration, we could confidently say that wealth issue and information issue remain as two of the most important factors behind young people's unemployment, since when they know what kind of jobs fit them and they have prepared well accordingly (with the help of wealth), they will get that sort of jobs. If young people have known (with the help of information) before they enter job market what are the expectations of employers, they will act accordingly and equip themselves with what employers want, such as engaging in a training seminar to develop more skills or paying for guidance on how to improve their performance during interviews. If so, they won't fail during recruitment and finally get a job. This is the power of wealth and information.

However, this doesn't mean that other factors do not play a role in young people's employment, and there are even many who do not have much wealth and with little information yet find proper jobs and have made great achievements in their career. This does not go contrary to the statement that youth unemployment problem reflects a lack wealth and information, since it is natural that various factors would affect employment prospect, with one key issue is the ability of youth. If he is a genius, or is much more capable than his peers, he would have no problem of finding a job and this has only a little relationship with the level of wealth and information that he possesses. But these are just individual cases, and when we examine youth unemployment problem from the perspective of the whole world, we would notice the role of these crucial factors: wealth and information.

While I do not give a specific data showing that to which extend wealth and information make a difference on young people's career prospect, we know that these two factors are common and critical, which are the most important ones and would guide our further analysis. Wealth and information play a crucial role in the developing of competencies of youth people, and the lack of wealth as well as information has led to the result that many youths are not qualified for their desired jobs. As a result, from the perspective of labor-supply, youth unemployment problem occurs because many youths are not competent enough for employment, which is a result of their lack of information and wealth.

5.5 Sources of wealth and information

Once roles of wealth and information in the existence of youth unemployment problem have been identified, the next step is to find out the sources of wealth and information, or in other words, where wealth comes from and where information comes from.

For young people, where does wealth come from?

There is an obvious answer to this question: family. For the majority of youth, they have no sources of income since they have no jobs—especially during periods when they are too young to work. And it is their parents or other family members that provide wealth to support them from their early days until later in their early adulthood.

Let's have a better understanding about this through the case of education, which MCG has provided some insights in their global surveys. When asked why they were not enrolled in post-secondary studies, on average 31% respondents replied that they couldn't afford to[76]. And except for youth from UK and Sweden, who could get abundant loan or financial support from government or other stakeholders, young people from France, Germany, Greece, Italy, Portugal and Spain generally reported self-funding or family support to be the primary method for paying the charges for their education or training[77]: 78% stated that they relied on self-funding or family support and only 22.6% respondents said they have support from government, education providers or employers, with a much lower portion, 15.5%, respondents saying they have scholarships.

Data above exhibit the situation relating to education, and when it comes to other issues such as living expenses or travelling expenses, the portion of self-funding and family support would certainly rise. Noticed that young people are generally too young to work, and then we could conclude that the primary source of wealth for young people are their families.

And how about information? For young people, where does information come from? Noticing that information here in this book mainly refers to the information that matters in youth unemployment issue, such as information concerning job market or labor issues, and includes which discipline to learn in university and so on.

In the two reports issued by MCG, they state that there is a gap of information between education providers and employers, and thus try to build an *Education to Employment(E2E) Highway* that could alleviate such gap. While there may exist such an information gap between education providers and employers, we could also observe the existence of information gap between another pair of stakeholders—the two sides of youth labor force: the supply side of youth labor and the demand side of youth labor. What's more, there is one crucial fact that is often neglected in the discussion of youth unemployment problem, a fact we must consider in order to build a comprehensive view of youth unemployment problem. This fact is that the unemployed youths, while there are plenty of them, actually constitute just a small portion of total youths, and there are much more youths who could get employment, with many of them getting pretty good ones.

For example, based on data in figure 2.2, we find that in the past 20 years the highest youth unemployment rate for the world as a whole happened in 2003, which was 14.37%. While this means around 14.37% of youth labor force having no jobs, it also means 85.63% of total youth labor have jobs. 85.63% is almost six times of 14.37%, and thus those who have jobs constitute a major portion of total youth labor.

If we think the information gap between two sides of youth labor has prevented many youths from getting jobs, we have to ask that why this information gap does not exist for a much larger group of youth? If information gap is a major cause of young people's unemployment, there must be no such gap for those who have jobs, and then to find out why there is no such gap for them will help us to understand why there exists information gap for those unemployed young people.

We are curious that, why there exists information gap for one group of young people yet doesn't exist for another group?

MCG proposes an explanation under their E2E highway framework, that's the delay of education system. When education providers do not react quickly about the change of needs of employers, what students learn in school will not match what employers expect from their newly recruited candidates, and McKinsey has suggested the lack of interaction between education providers and employers contributing to the formation of information gap.

This explanation is a typical point of view to understand the existing of information gap, while it is helpful, it has one drawback, that is couldn't explain the fact that when we look at youth unemployment problem from the perspective of total youth, there is no such information gap for most of them.

If there is information gap between education providers and employers, why would much more youths face no such gap (since they have jobs)? Generally speaking, there isn't a perfect 100% student placement rate even for those top schools in the world and thus for the majority of education providers, the employment rate of their fresh graduates would be lower than 100%. If there is information gap between education and employment, and this information gap would lead to unemployment, and then we must ask why most students would have jobs while some other students graduated from the same school have no jobs?

This puzzle has led us to examine information gap from a new perspective: not the perspective of institutions but that of individuals. In fact, when we focus on information gap between the supply side of youth labor force (young people) and the demand side of youth labor force (employers), we could find that, there is actually one bridge that connects two sides of youth labor force. This bridge has enabled the exchange of information between two sides of youth labor, and specifically, let information flow from side of employers to the side of young people.

What is this bridge?

This powerful bright isn't mysterious at all, which are young people's parents. The key point is that as adults, young people's parents are employed in job market. On one hand, parents bring up their children and guide them; on the other hand, these parents, as adults, have jobs in the job market. Employed people could get access to information from job market, and through their messages, information on the employer side flows to the youth side. There are also adults who don't have jobs, and they possess no information or limited information on job market, and as a result their children would get less information on side of labor demand through the intermediary of their parents. The fact that some adults having jobs while others not explains why there is information gap for many youths while there is no such gap for much more youth.

There is an old saying called the duck knows first when the river becomes warm in spring, with the rationale being that ducks spend their time in the river, and when the temperature of water in the river rises as spring comes, they will notice this change more quickly than other creatures living on the land. This rationale could be applied to our discussion of information gap here: compared with those who don't have jobs, those who have jobs will have better knowledge concerning changes in job market, and when they transmit this kind of information to their children, these children are then better informed and there comes a narrowed information gap for them.

Young people are just too young to have experience and knowledge about job market, and when schools do not provide them with such information, they could only obtain from their parents, or other relatives. The amount and quality of information transmitted by their parents vary, and the amount and quality of information that young people receive vary, which explains why there is significant information gap for many youths while not for others.

While there is no direct evidence in current materials, we do find clues of this hypothesis. For example, in MCG's second report, there is one exhibit showing that among those who attend post-secondary education, different groups of youth possess different levels of information on job market opportunities[78]. From that exhibit, we find on average 45.4% of total youth know their family's opinion on what discipline they should learn in university, a percentage that is large enough to declare its role. Besides, based on the same exhibit, we find discrepancy between different segments of youth, with generally 49% High Achievers[i] know their family's opinion yet only 40% Dreamers know that. All these data indicate that information from family members is different for different segments of youth, and generally is positively related to their career prospects. While these data do not show us that information gap for young people relates to their parents' employment situation, we do know that information gap is more severe for some youths while less severe for others, and this difference relates to family.

Besides, in the same report the authors say that the well-positioned segment of youth, the segment enjoying the best employment status and being "well informed and caring about their educational options and future", consists of mainly older (aged of 26-29) and wealthier youth. The fact of being older would possess more information doesn't go contrary to the conclusion just now, since at a younger age, people's

---

[i] Based on instructions in MCG's report, high achievers refer to those youths who are focused, make best of support they receive, and are considered as in better condition than dreamers, who could only wish they had known more so that they could have made better decisions to reach their ambitions

information on job market mainly comes from their parents or other family members, and as they grow older and become more experienced, they will be able to get access to other sources of information, such as learning through their internship experience, through taking part in professional training classes, or simply through talking to friends who possess such information. However, the fact of information gap narrows as young people grow older wouldn't help too much for young people's unemployment, since the value of information relates to the time point that people obtain such information, and the late coming of information for many youths as they grow older may simply make these pieces of information useless[i].

Now people may wonder that how could adults' having jobs narrow the information gap for their children? This question makes sense, since there are so many industries and each industry have some unique characteristics. And inside one company, there are different roles and even for the same role in the same company, there are different levels of positions. All these make it impossible for one person in job market to hold enough information on every aspects of job market. Thus, I must clarify that I state information gap disappears or narrows for those whose parents have jobs, doesn't necessarily mean that those children hold adequate information about job market and know specific information of the characteristics and requirements of different types of jobs. Instead, to possess information on job market mainly refers to the situation that the youth know the general rules of job market, such as it is important be punctual and show work ethic, and fully realize the fact that there is difference between work environment and school or home. For those well-informed, they know they need to explore and get prepared for employment—for example, a student who wants to enter consulting industry would actively gather information on the requirements of consultants and develop their skills concerning case interviews.

Information gap between young people and employers does not relate to specific types of jobs or specific requirements to detail, but in fact, relates more to the general sense of being at work. Even though people in different jobs possess different skills and have professional habits, they share the same sense of being at work, which means they know when they are at work that they should behave differently compared with when they are at home, and sometimes may behave against their own will. The rules of home environment are totally different from those of work environment, and only if people respect and follow the rules of work environment could they make progress continually in

---

[i] I will discuss more about information's time issue in chapter 6

their career.

In this sense, the information gap caused by parents' different employment status mainly refers to some general things, for which we have obtained two indirect evidences —when I state indirect evidence, I mean that concerning the conclusion, these evidences are more likely to support it rather than denying it.

One indirect evidence is the survey of MCG, in which there is one question pointing out the expected skills favored by employers, and the top four skills are work ethic, teamwork, local language and oral communication, which don't relate to any specific type of roles, but mainly relate to some overall and general traits. The second indirect evidence is the fact that even if some people would enter their ideal industries when they first step into job market, most people would enter a suboptimal industry at the beginning of their career and change their jobs later. This is a common situation, since whether one could get the job that he desires largely depends on external factors, which is full of uncertainties, and thus even if they have the right set of skills, they may still miss their targets if the industry they desire do not need entry-level employees at the time they enter job market. The key point of this second evidence is that people just cannot possess perfect information on job market, and so does the information that children obtain from their parents.

To conclude, just as wealth, information generally comes from family members and now, we know that for young people, the main source of wealth and information is the same: their parents, or families.

5.6 Family: another stakeholder in youth unemployment analysis

We already know that wealth and information matter in young people's employment and for them, wealth and information mainly come from family members, and thus the aspect of family must also be included in youth unemployment analysis.

Wealth issue is easy to understand, and when we try to understand the information gap for young people, we take the whole youth into consideration. Rather than following the traditional approach of just focusing on the unemployed youth and wondering why they lack information, we are also curious about why much more youths have jobs, which indicates their not lacking of information. When conduct analysis in this way, causes of youth unemployment problem become more distinct and the role of family emerges.

The analysis of youth unemployment in this book bases on the philosophy that takes other factors as given and focuses on the youth themselves to find causes of youth unemployment. And up to now, our analysis points out that youth unemployment rate is high because many youths do not meet requirements of employers[i], which occurs as a result of these youth's lack of wealth and information. At this point, our analysis needs to continue, since our understanding now is just sort of a cross-section analysis: our attention concentrates too much on the time that young people leave school seeking employment.

But we know, *Rome wasn't built in a day*, and these facts that we have observed—young people cannot find jobs for their lack of competences are just consequences, reasons of which lie in the past, long before young people entering job market to seek employment. The building of skills requires time, which may be years of time, so as the preparation for employment, both mentally and technically. As a result, we also need to understand the occurring of youth unemployment based on the dimension of time, which becomes possible by introducing family into our analysis.

	Stage-one	Stage-two	Stage-three
People's status	Childhood	Growing up	Seeking employment
Stakeholder(s) involved	Family	Education providers & Family	Employers

Table 5.2 Three stages in young people's pre-adulthood life

Table 5.2 illustrates briefly the idea that there are different stages in young people's pre-adulthood life, and in each stage main stakeholders involved are different. To include the dimension of family in our analysis enables us to fill in the stakeholder in the first stage, since at this stage people are simply too young to go to school, not to mention to go to work. In stage two, children spend large amount of time learning at school, during which period family also plays a role. And in stage three, young people leave school to seek employment, which is crucial for their

---

[i] Notice that this book doesn't take into consideration the situation that labor supply exceeds labor demand

later life. Today's youth unemployment crisis we've observed now occurs in stage three for the youth, but we know, consequences in stage three relate to things happened in stage two and even stage one—we will discuss more about this in the next chapter.

Whether it is intended or not, the role of family has been neglected in many researchers' youth unemployment analyses, but we now acknowledge that we must include family in our analysis, otherwise we won't be able to continue our analysis based on the dimension of time. Education could also be considered as a component of time-dimension analysis, but our philosophy in this book is that we consider youth unemployment problem as the problem of young people, rather than problem of other stakeholders, and we are not going to discuss how educational system should be revised to tackle youth unemployment. Traditionally, the youth and their families are considered as one stakeholder, but in this book, I will separate them from each other since they've played different roles in the occurring of youth unemployment crisis.

5.7 Consistency between the possession of wealth and information

Up to now, the logic of my youth unemployment analysis is as follows: youth unemployment rate rises because many youths do not meet requirements of employers, or equally, they are not believed to be competent enough for employment. And the reason behind these youths' incompetency is their lack of wealth and information. For young people, wealth and information mainly come from family members, and thus these youths' unemployment occurs as a result of their families' lack of wealth and information. The conclusion is that young people's having jobs or not generally reflects the difference in levels of wealth and information that their families possess.

While wealth is relatively concrete, which could be easily measured by currency, information is quite a broad concept and is hard to be summarized. Here in this book, we confine information as messages relating to employment and job market, and thus such information derives from people's experience in job market—their jobs. Here we link the possession of information with people's employment status, and we could understand this from two aspects: one is from the difference among levels of employment within companies and the other is from the difference among companies in different industries.

Within a specific firm, as one person moves to a higher position, the information he possesses and could get access to will also increase, since when he takes more responsibility, he will need to think from a broader perspective. For example, when he is an entry-level employee, all he needs to care about is to do his job well. But when he has been promoted and is in charge of one department, he has to care about other people in the department, and also the interaction between his department and other departments. And when he becomes one member of top management team of the firm, he will begin to think about things from the perspective of whole firm, which may also requires taking into consideration the movement of external environment. As such, we could say that top management team possess more information relating to job market than their employees.

Similar to the situation within companies, people work in different industries will possess different kinds of information too. For example, people work in hotel industries will care about different things compared with people work in investment banking industries. While there are two aspects to link information difference with people's employment, I suggest the information difference within one firm should be highlighted. This means information difference between people working in different industries will be less important for the discussion of youth unemployment compared with information difference between different levels of positions within one firm.

Not just information, wealth actually relates to people's employment too. Based on data in figure 8.7 and 8.8 of Thomas Piketty's bestseller *Capital in the 21th century*, we find in US, starting from 1970s the expansion of wage inequality has played a major role in the rising inequality of income, and the increase of income for top 1% population in the US has mainly benefited from their increase of wages. Besides, in the year 2007 of US, only for the income of top 0.1% population, capital income contributes more than labor income.[79]

In fact, we could make a step further and also consider the relationship between wealth and employment from two aspects: one is within one firm and the other exists between firms. Professor of Stanford University, Nicholas Bloom (2017) has conducted research on this area and found that income inequality between firms plays a larger role than within firms[80]. This means different employment status between firms contributes more to people's wealth status than different employment status within firms.

Now we have found the relationship between information and employment and the relationship between wealth and employment, and we cannot help wondering, could employment perform as an agent, so that the status of information would link to the status of wealth? I mean, for those who lack wealth and information, if the lack of wealth and the lack of information exist for the same reason (employment status), and thus the level of wealth possessed would be generally the same as the level of information possessed, the lack of both could be integrated as one: lack of wealth. If so, youth unemployment problem actually happens as a result of wealth inequality problem.

To verify this, we need first to ask a question: Could employment status perform as the agent that connects information and wealth?

While we have already known that both information and wealth relate to employment, we have also known both of them are connected with employment in two ways: within the same firm and between different firms. However, we have concluded that information differences relate more to employment within the same firms whereas wealth differences relate more to employment between different firms. If so, employment cannot perform as the agent that connects wealth and information.

Luckily, we have found an important misunderstanding here. We state a lack of information and wealth has caused many youths unable to get employment, we mean an absolute short of information and wealth is the reason. And here we state that differences of information and wealth between adults relate to their employment, we refer to a relative figure. There is an obvious difference between an absolute figure and a relative one: the absolute level of one thing doesn't relate to the difference between two things. For example, when information and wealth that everyone possesses is equal yet inadequate, then all the youth will have higher possibility of unemployment for a lack of information and wealth. On the contrary, when information and wealth that everyone possesses is highly divergent yet all of them are above a certain necessary level, then all the youth will have lower risk of unemployment since all of them do not suffer from the lack of information and wealth.

As a result, for youth unemployment, what matters more is the absolute short of information and wealth, rather than differences between people, and thus information could link to wealth through the intermediary of employment, since both information and wealth relates to employment, whether within firms or between firms. In fact, this statement is strengthened by the fact that for those who have jobs and those who do not have jobs, the consistency between wealth and information becomes more solid, since without jobs, people have few sources of income and have few channels to obtain information on jobs market. All these mean that those who lack wealth tend to be short of information too.

Since the lack of wealth is actually accompanied with a lack of information, young people's lack of wealth and lack of information could generally be summarized as one thing: lack of wealth. However, as have been mentioned that information relates more to differences within firms while wealth relates more to differences between firms, the consistency between the possession of information and wealth is not so robust and there may exists mismatch between the two of them—we will discuss more about this in chapter 7. Here in our analysis, the bottom line is that the possession of information could be considered to be consistent with the possession of wealth, and then the lack of information and the lack of wealth could be summarized as a lack of wealth.

5.8 Youth unemployment and wealth inequality

The fact that different families possess different levels of wealth and information, helps to explain differences in competencies between young people when they seek employment. Those who are unemployed tend to be those who possess less wealth and information, and in view of the idea that the lack of information is generally consistent with a lack of wealth, we would conclude that youth unemployment problem actually reflects a long-discussed issue: wealth inequality. When we move a step further, incorporating one key assumption of this book, that there are enough job opportunities for the youth, we would find that there is actually no youth unemployment problem, and the problem behind all those phenomena is wealth inequality: when the level of wealth and information that everyone possesses reaches above a certain level, there would be no youth unemployment problem.

Here we state that youth unemployment problem happens as a result of wealth inequality, but this doesn't mean it is the level of gap between the richest and the poorest that determines the level of youth unemployment rate. Instead, we have used descriptions as "a lack of wealth" to represent the relationship between wealth and unemployment and thus the key point is that there is a threshold, and when the level of wealth possessed by someone reaches above this threshold, he will have a much lower possibility of unemployment. And thus, while we use the description of "wealth inequality", the idea we actually mean is an absolute value that similar to the concept of "absolute poverty", and it is this "absolute" level of wealth that relates to youth unemployment rate: as the level of wealth for more people falls below this absolute level, youth unemployment rate rises.

This judgment has obtained evidence from economic data, which is shown in four scatter diagrams presented below. These four scatterplots consist of six sets of data that relate to wealth inequality and youth unemployment, which include GINI coefficient, poverty rate, child poverty rate, poverty gap, wealth gap and youth unemployment rate. All these data come from OECD website[81,82], where readers could also find the definition and description of these indicators.

Indicator of wealth inequality	Definition	Year of data
Poverty Rate	Also called Relative Income Poverty and is the percentage of people whose income falls below the national poverty line, which is half of the median household income of the total population [83]. Noticed that "income" here refers to disposable income and has been adjusted for the size of household.	2014
Child Poverty Rate	This is the poverty rate of those 0-17 year-old, which is calculated based on an equalized household disposable income.[84]	2014
Poverty Gap	This is "the ratio by which the mean income of the poor falls below the poverty line." [85] And the definition of the poor is the same as that of poverty rate calculation.	2014
Wealth gap	This is what I use to represent a term that I found on the website of OECD, called top 20% vs. bottom 20%, and is "the average income of the top 20% as a multiple of the average income of bottom 20% of the income scale."[86]	2014

Figure 5.1 A brief illustration of four indicators of wealth inequality

Here I will just give a brief illustration (based on the description on OECD website) of four measurements of wealth inequality, which are shown in figure 5.1.

Due to data availability, I only present data of seven countries: Germany, Greece, France, Portugal, Spain, Sweden, and United Kingdom. These seven countries are all developed ones, which share similarities in many

Youth unemployment and wealth inequality

key aspects, and this makes them comparable with each other concerning the relationship between wealth inequality and youth unemployment. Besides, in order to represent the causal relationship between wealth inequality and youth unemployment problem, I have used one-year lag data of youth unemployment rate compared to those wealth inequality indicators, and since youth unemployment rate is obtained of the year 2015, wealth inequality indicators are set for the year of 2014. One-year lag is not a precise measurement but will reflect the relationship between wealth inequality and youth unemployment rate to some degree.

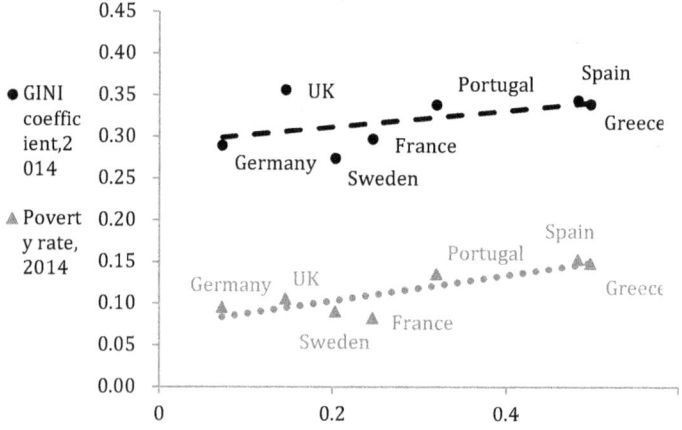

Figure 5.2 GINI Coefficient, poverty rate and youth unemployment rate

Youth unemployment and wealth inequality

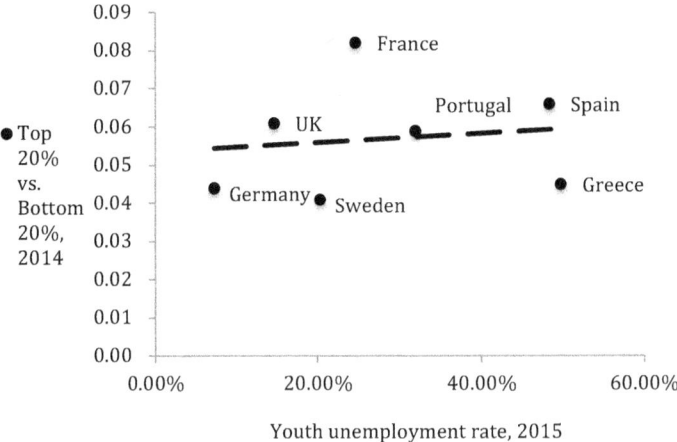

Figure 5.3 Wealth gap and youth unemployment rate

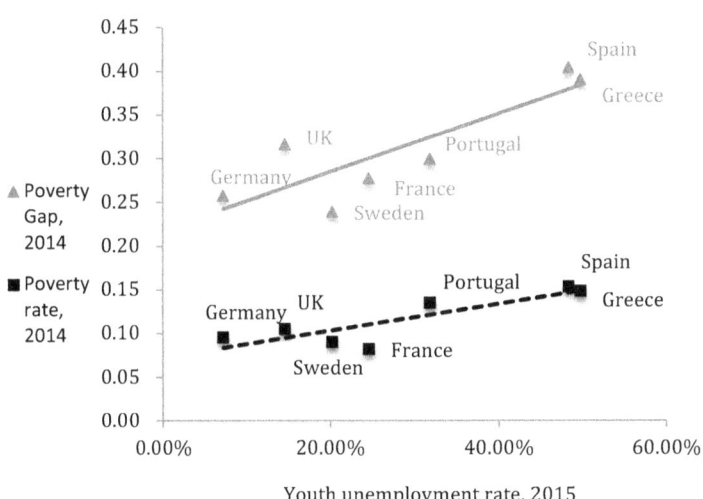

Figure 5.4 Poverty rate, poverty gap and youth unemployment rate

Youth unemployment and wealth inequality

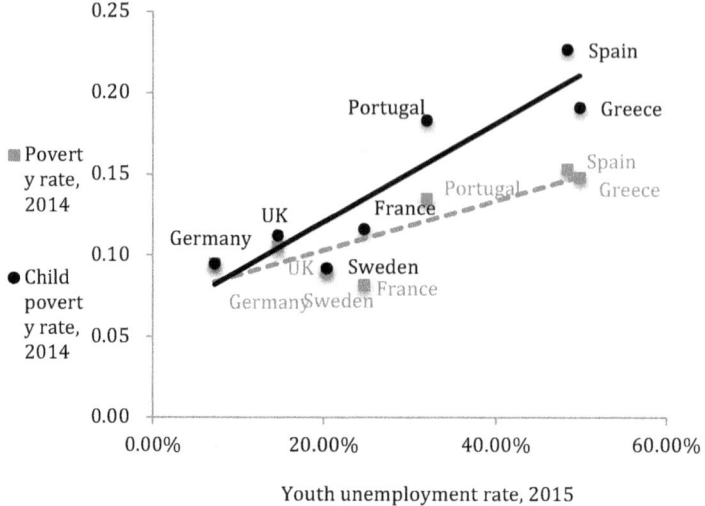

Figure 5.5 Poverty rate, child poverty rate and youth unemployment rate

From figure 5.2 we could find that one-year lag youth unemployment rate is positive related to both GINI coefficient and poverty rate, and this relationship is more likely to be stable for poverty rate since all points are quite close to the trend line. For GINI coefficient, the revealed positive relationship is less likely to be robust, since compared to poverty rate, points of GINI coefficient and youth unemployment rate stay relatively far from the trend line.

GINI coefficient reflects the difference between the rich and the poor whereas poverty rate reflects the absolute lack of wealth of the poor[i], and thus figure 5.2 reminds us that for youth unemployment issue, what matters more is the absolute lack of wealth of the poor, rather than the relative difference between the rich and the poor. This statement is strengthened by the fact revealed in figure 5.3 that the relationship between wealth gap and youth unemployment rate is not obvious. What's more, all points are located dispersedly around the trend line, and this makes it less likely to conclude that there is causal relationship between youth unemployment rate and wealth difference between the very rich and very poor.

---

[i] Even though poverty rate itself is a kind of relative measurement

Figure 5.4 shows the scatterplots of poverty rate, poverty gap and youth unemployment rate. As we can see, it seems that youth unemployment rate relates more to poverty gap than poverty rate, but points representing poverty gap are more dispersedly located around the trend line, and this makes the relationship between poverty gap and youth unemployment rate less effective. And figure 5.5 is the scatterplots of poverty rate, child poverty rate and youth unemployment rate. Just as poverty gap, child poverty rate seems relates more to youth unemployment rate. This is reasonable, since youth unemployment rate focuses on the employment situation of those aged between 15 and 24, and thus poverty rate of the total population would be a less important factor than child poverty rate.

Diagrams above reflect the relationship between youth unemployment rate and wealth equality, especially the absolute lack of wealth of the poor rather than the difference between the very rich and very poor. The implication of this finding is that to tackle youth unemployment problem, what we need to do first is to help the poor become less poor, rather than to make the rich less rich.

Noticing that the relationship revealed between youth unemployment rate and wealth inequality is not perfect, and this is partly because the analysis of this book is built on the assumption that there are enough job opportunities, which is not typically true for most countries, especially when we realize that the movement of business cycle such as the period of expansion or the period of recession will definitely increase or reduce jobs available for the youth. Besides, while these seven countries share many similarities, they are different in many other aspects, and youth unemployment situation is highly related to one country's policy environment. This has reduced the effectiveness of indicators of these countries for comparison purpose. Now let's make it clear: when I state youth unemployment problem relating to wealth inequality, I mean in each country the poor tend to have higher youth unemployment rate compared with the rich, or in other words, the poor suffer more from youth unemployment problem than the rich.

Besides economic data, I have also found supports of this statement from facts observed in job market.

One important fact relates to the negative relationship between education level and youth unemployment rate. Data tell us that tertiary education brings positive return and as the level of education increases, rate of youth unemployment falls. And, the level of education is strongly related to wealth status. When we consider youth categories[i] like "no interest" or "do not believe education's value" exist as a result of their lack of information, the relationship between education level and wealth status would grow even stronger. For young people, wealth and information mainly come from family members, and their lack of wealth and information reflects the status of their family's lack of wealth and information, and then the phenomenon that some youths have jobs while others not happen as a result of wealth inequality.

Another fact derives from one reasoning based on MCG's global survey. One question of their survey provides employers' perception about their new-hire's level of preparation, and these responded employers come from various sectors[87]. When we look through the result[ii], we find newly recruited young people working in education, financial intermediation, and health & social work industries are better prepared than young people working in hotels & restaurants, agriculture, hunting, forestry & fishing, and wholesale & retail trade industries. Taking into consideration the fact that the former three industries tend to have higher threshold (require longer period of education, and typically require an advanced degree such as master's degree or doctor's degree) than the latter three, we must ask that why would candidates seeking for jobs that require larger efforts of preparation tend to be better prepared than those seeking for jobs that only require shorter periods of preparation?

We could find a reasonable explanation about this following the logic that youth unemployment problem happens as result of wealth inequality problem.

Those industries with higher thresholds tend to have stable career prospect and generally higher income than those with lower thresholds, and more children from the richer families will prefer to work in the former three kinds of industries. Since they can get access to adequate wealth and information, they are able to develop their skills and competencies accordingly, and this is why these industries are less affected by youth unemployment crisis. For the poor, they have fewer opportunities to finish high level of education which is typically a must for applying for jobs in those sectors with higher thresholds, and the percentage of them applying for low threshold industries such as agriculture will be larger than for high threshold industries like health care, and thus employers from sector with lower thresholds would find their new-recruit less prepared.

---

[i] For more information, please refer to Table 5.1
[ii] For a brief illustration, please refer to table 4.2

A larger share of the rich would choose sectors that have higher entry thresholds for the pursuit of more stable career prospect and a larger share of the poor would choose sectors that have lower entry thresholds. Since the rich have adequate wealth and information, they could prepare well for their employment, but this is not the case of the poor, who are less prepared for their lack of wealth and information. And this leads to the result that even though industries with higher thresholds are relatively demanding yet have a larger proportion of better prepared candidates.

5.9 Issues concerning the relationship between wealth and unemployment

There will be a lot of discussions about the relationship between youth unemployment problem and wealth inequality problem, and just one side of the relationship—wealth inequality has already aroused endless debate. Here targeting at this relationship, I will present only three questions and they are stated as below.

Question 1: If youth unemployment problem exists as a result of wealth inequality (or many people's lack of wealth), why would it appear in the recent decades while wealth inequality problem has persisted in the history of human being?
This inconsistency is mainly due to changes on the side of youth labor demand.

In the long history, there wasn't youth unemployment problem because there was relatively larger youth labor demand compared with youth labor supply, but this situation changed gradually in the last century. After World War 2, the third revolution in science and technology has greatly promoted the advancement of productivity, and many jobs on assembly line have been replaced by machines—a trend has been continuing since then. On one hand, the amount of labor demand is reduced and on the other hand, for existing job opportunities, requirements have been raised—this is especially true when we realize that jobs are more diversified, and meantime more specialized. What's more, globalization has greatly promoted the flow of production factors including labor force, and for developed areas such as Europe, inflows of foreign-born labors have taken up some job opportunities—while this may not get reflected on unemployment rate since unemployment between native labor and foreign-born labor are largely the same, inflow of labor force do affect labor demand of local youth in a way that goes against their will.

In short, in the past decades there have been dramatic changes on the side of youth labor demand and compared with the rich who are able to detect such changes and then prepare accordingly, the poor are less aware of those changes for their lack of wealth and information. This has made young people especially the poor less prepared for employment challenges on job market, which brings about youth unemployment problem.

But this doesn't contradict the focus of this book—that to analyze the reasons as well as solutions of youth unemployment problem from the perspective of labor supply. This is because the advancement of science and technology is an irreversible trend and so is the process of globalization, the youth could only adapt in order to succeed. Besides, just as has been stressed in chapter 3, those factors on labor demand such as economic cycles are too unpredictable to count on, and if we move a step further, that employment is not only the right of young people but also their duty, we would find young people should become more competent—future conditions on job market rely on today's youths.

Question 2: Having jobs or not is a binary variable—yes or no, but the amount of wealth is a continuous variable, which means there are different levels of wealth. How could we match a binary variable with a continuous one?

Indeed, the problem that this book targets at is a binary situation, but under the assumption that there are enough job opportunities[i], the statement that youth unemployment problem is part of wealth inequality or the lack of wealth and information has led many youths unprepared for employment does not mean if household income falls below a certain level, children from these families will certainly not be able to find employment. There is no such clear and definite relationship between wealth status and young people's unemployment, rather, the actual relationship is that the lack of wealth and information will increase young people's probability of unemployment, and thus youth unemployment rate of the poor is higher than that of the rich, which means the poor suffer more than the rich from youth unemployment problem.

This is an attempt of finding causes as well as solutions of youth unemployment problem from the perspective of labor supply, which will contribute to the understanding of key issues such as who is

---

[i] As is illustrate in section 3.6, this is a reasonable assumption

unemployed, why are they unemployed and what we should do in order to help them get employed. In fact, while young people's employment prospects relate to their possessing of wealth and information, this doesn't explain the whole story of youth unemployment since young people's employment also relate to many other factors, such as business cycles, policy environment, and personal traits including health status. In other words, there are many uncertainties in young people's employment prospect and the extreme situation of unemployment doesn't necessarily link to a certain level of wealth and information.

In fact, while unemployment is an extreme situation, this doesn't mean having jobs is always better than having no jobs and some forms of employment may be quite close to unemployment. For example, being at internship or taking up a temporary job[i] are considered as having a job, but such kinds of employment status do not provide a decent career prospect. These kinds of job types, while recorded as employment, couldn't provide young people a prosperous career prospect for the instability of employment and low speed of developing skill, and thus contribute little to young people's long-term career ambition, or their expectation of becoming more skilled and obtaining better welfare as they grow older. If so, employment status is actually not a binary variable.

Question 3: Does the relationship between wealth inequality and youth unemployment reveal an alternative solution of wealth inequality problem?

Since youth unemployment problem could be considered as part of wealth inequality problem, there exists interaction between the two of them: youth unemployment is not just a result of wealth inequality but will reinforce wealth inequality and thus is one cause of wealth inequality. As a result, the answer to question 3 would be: yes.

The younger generation of the poor tend to have less probability of finding employment and the chances of those youths becoming rich would also be smaller. If they are not rich, their children—the grandchildren generation of the originally poor, tend to have higher unemployment rate, and lead them to stay poor. Under this process, through generations the poor will more likely to remain poor. And this is a different case for the rich. Children of the rich tend to have less risk of unemployment since they are better prepared, and thus they are more likely to remain rich. When they are rich, their children—the grandchildren of the first generation, would have less danger of

---

[i] Vulnerable forms of employment

unemployment, which would keep their status of being rich. And this is why the rich would have large possibilities of remaining rich through generations.

Following the logic shown above, on one hand the rich remains rich and perhaps richer, on the other hand the poor remains poor and maybe poorer—wealth inequality situation persists, possibly strengthens. However, this logic could also be reverted if children of the poor get jobs. When the younger generations of the poor have jobs, they are more likely to become rich and if they are rich, their children—the grandchildren generation of the originally poor are more likely to have employment, which would keep their status of being rich. Through generations, when the rich remains rich and the poor becomes rich, wealth inequality will become less important, especially concerning the absolute poverty of the poor.

ILO has stressed a similar opinion in their report, *World Employment and Social Outlook 2016: Transforming Jobs to End Poverty*[88], but largely focused on promoting "decent employment". And in one of their latest reports, *World Employment and Social Outlook: Trends 2017*[89], ILO stresses the phenomenon of working poverty. According to the report, working poverty is expected to be 28.7% for emerging and developing countries in 2017, and in the same year, 1.4 billion people are expected to work in vulnerable forms of employment globally, which is around 42% of total employment.

While vulnerable employment and working poverty remain a concern, people in these conditions are better than those who have no jobs—who are even poorer. On the way towards good employment as well as ending poverty, any improvement is worthy and thus to help young people find jobs—even if vulnerable ones, will contribute to the ease of wealth inequality problem.

6. INFORMATION ASYMMETRY, SIGNALS AND THE DIMENSION OF TIME

6.1 Trace backwards into the past

In general circumstances, when unemployment rate has risen too much, the first thought would be to stimulate economy so as to create more job positions. However, when it is youth unemployment that we come across, this approach may not be as reasonable as it is used to be.

The logic of creating more jobs when unemployment rate rises has an underlying assumption that there is limited number of job opportunities available for job seekers. This might be true for adults, but for the youth, we have a good reason to doubt its reliability. It is widely accepted that young people are not experienced and are short of specialized skills, and thus employers would only expect some kinds of common skills from them, which enables young people to apply for many different types of positions. As a result, a lack of job positions is not the whole story of youth unemployment analysis.

Based on former discussions of this book, we know that young people—the side of labor supply, should also be responsible for their unemployment. As a result, when we are dealing with youth unemployment problem, we need to jump out of the traditional zone that highlights job creation. What makes this especially important is the consideration that for young people, their entering job market to find jobs is not only a start—start of a new life stage, but also an end—the end showing us how well they have prepared for their employment, or how hardworking they were in the past. And thus, the reasons for their unemployment may not occur during the time that they seek employment, but much earlier before they enter job market.

When deal with youth unemployment problem, too much attention has been paid to current conditions and current situations, but if the causes of youth unemployment problem lie in the past that before the youth entering job market, focusing too much on the time when they enter job market may miss the point. As such, if the causes of youth unemployment exist before the youth entering job market, our intervention should also be carried out before the youth entering job market. Remember that we have used an example of river to illustrate the rationality of time consideration in chapter 2.

If a river gets polluted from upstream, it would be ineffective and too costly just trying to purify the river downstream at the mouth, since contaminated water will come endlessly. Instead, we should trace backwards along the river and find the factory that keeps pouring wasted water into the river. If we could set up purifying facilities within the factory and thus wasted water would be first purified before flowing into the river, we could conquer this problem effectively and permanently. Now we come across youth unemployment problem, and the methods of creating more job positions are similar to the efforts of setting up cleaning facilities at downstream of the river, which does help in the short run—in a cost ineffective way and may not be a permanent solution.

This book has tried to look beyond current situation to examine the topic of youth unemployment problem, and if the causes of incompetency of the youth do not lie in the time that they step into job market, but lying in their growing process or the process that they receive education, it would be insufficient to just create more job positions, since in the future, there would be also youths with weak competencies entering job market to seek employment. We would never be able to provide enough jobs for those youths, just as we would never be able to purify the river downstream when the river is polluted upstream.

Besides, if we take into consideration the fact that there are uncertainties of when youth unemployment crisis will burst out and there exists time-lag between the time that we realize many youths having no jobs and the time that more jobs are provided, the approach of creating jobs when unemployment rate rises would be less effective and may bring about more problems. For example, thanks for the large-scale apprenticeship mechanisms, youth unemployment rate for UK has been declining significantly since 2012, from 21.2% in that year to 13.0% in 2016[90]. But other problems emerge such as in Nov. 2017, the warning illustrated by news titled *Britain's Debt Will Not Fall to 2008 Levels Until 2060s, IFS Says in Startling Warning*[91]. If the words of Paul Johnson in the article are trustworthy, that UK has a high possibility of losing earnings growth for consecutive two decades, then we must wonder, what if youth unemployment rate for UK rises again? And when youth unemployment crisis bursts out again, would UK have enough funding to carry out another round of boosting apprenticeships?

This book focuses on reasons of young people themselves and highlights an active approach to deal with youth unemployment: to trace back into the past long before young people entering job market, and to find out why would many youths are not qualified for employment so that we could intervene early for the future generations. Following this approach, the dimension of time should also be included in the analysis of youth unemployment problem.

If we consider that to work is not only the right of young people but also their duty, and if more youths are competent for employment, prospect of the overall economy would become better. Are there any things happened in the past that have prevented young people from getting employment?

6.2 Possessing university degree shows positive signal for recruiters

Let's come back to the case that I introduced in section 4.1, which tells us the fact that there would be a factor relating to education experience in almost any types of recruitment advertisements, and many jobs are only open for those who possess college degrees. How could we understand this? Is it as simple as having no experience of studying in university? Or equally, is it as simple as not possessing a college degree? How could we understand this type of unemployment?

It is difficult to find answers of these questions directly, and let's consider an alternative question: why would a college degree matter so much for some recruiters during their recruitment?

Let's simplify this new question and consider two candidates competing for the same position: one has a college degree while the other doesn't, but all other things remain the same for these two candidates, including but not limited to personal traits, motivation, internship experience and even scores of standardized languages tests. Which candidate to choose? For most recruiters, this is not a difficult decision, and the one with a college degree would become the chosen one.

Why? Because a college degree indicates a lot of positive things: a successful student in the college entrance competition several years ago, having received systematic training and education in certain areas, having been exposed to different people in different activities, and also the alumni network. All these positive things carried by a college degree show recruiters the competences of the candidate, which would be a great competitive advantage for him to succeed in his career. The role that a college degree plays during recruitment is like a signal, a signal that tells recruiters this candidate possessing certain competitiveness that recruiters need.

In fact, not only employers need such signals during their recruitment, in many other activities we could also find the role of signals. As a result, not only individuals but also institutions are keen to acquire things that convey positive signals.

For example, business schools typically endeavor to win EQUIS accreditation, AACSB accreditation or both of them, since such recognitions would show the general public an overall world-class high-quality education institution. Once acquired such certifications, businesses schools tend to rank better in different kinds of ranking lists, to use the labels of such certifications in their advertisements to attract talented students and to establish more cooperative relationship with companies. The role of an EQUIS or AACSB accreditation plays for business schools is much like the role of a college degree plays for job seekers: they indicate positive things favored by the public.

Many things would send signals to people—whether be good signals or bad signals, and signals are prevailing in our human society, since we need them to assist us to make decision in a circumstance that is full of imperfect information and information asymmetry.

6.3 Information asymmetry and the role of signals

Signals play a crucial role in our human society, which is partly because of Information Asymmetry. Information asymmetry typically refers to the situation that one party in a transaction has information advantage over the other party, and the party with information advantage sometimes would distort the transaction in favor of his own benefits. Information asymmetry is such a common phenomenon in our society that many theories and topics are proposed based on it, such as adverse selection and the principal-agent problem.

When it comes to recruitment, we could also find the existence of information asymmetry. For recruiters of a company, job applicants—these fresh graduates in our topic of youth unemployment analysis, are completely unfamiliar and could be considered as strangers. Recruiters have no pre-existing acknowledgment about how competitive these candidates are and why they are applying for their company. What has made this situation worse is that even these young people themselves may not know their competitiveness, skills, advantages and disadvantages as well as their motivations very well. It's just that companies need more employees and fresh graduates need jobs—however difficult it is, recruiters must select some people.

This is where signals help. Signals represent a standardized third-parity opinion, which provides clear information telling recruiters what kind a person the candidate is and how competitive he is. And due to their highly-recognized accreditation procedure and well-established reputation, information carried by those signals is widely accepted among different groups of people, especially between strangers. Signals are essentially simple things that could be easily understood and readily accepted by different people, just as people from different cultures know smile means the same thing—friendly, even if they have no idea about the languages of other cultures. The result is that signals improve the efficiency of communication between unfamiliar people significantly.

Let's understand this by a simple sample. Language tests such as TOEFL and IELTS are kinds of standardized third party opinions, scores of which are widely accepted all over the world by universities, research institutions, companies and even governments as a measure of English competencies of exam takers—while these tests may not be able to provide a complete illustration of candidates' English abilities, they do provide a relatively comprehensive picture of candidates' English skills and thus contribute to the selection of people who are supposed to master English to a certain level.

Besides these language tests, standardized and widely recognized signals also include university degrees, university transcripts, professional certificates such as CFA or FRM, or the AACSB and EQUIS accreditations that we have mentioned in the former section. And in fact, signal is such a broad and open concept that includes not only standard tests, but also nonstandard stuffs such as specific experience of people. For example, when we are told that a person once reached the peak of Himalayas, summit of Mount Everest, we would quickly realize that this guy must be physically strong, otherwise he could never bear the atrocious weather of Himalayas. Besides, we may also conclude that this guy is mentally strong, otherwise he wouldn't be able to handle unexpected changes during his journey.

Experience that could be considered as signals has such a characteristic that when we notice it, we would come up with some opinions, and these opinions typically mean the same thing for the general public—just as the judgments that we have made about the Himalayas hiking case. As a result, these personalized stories and experience could also provide signals, based on which we would form some ideas about those people who have that kind of experience. For the purpose of understanding the role and importance of these stories, we describe them using one name: signals. From this point of view, anything that carries readily-accepted messages could be considered as signals, based on which we could have a better understanding about unfamiliar people.

Due to information asymmetry and information imperfection, it is both time-consuming and cost-demanding to make the right decision and this is why signals are welcomed, since signals would enable decision makers to obtain the information that they need to make their decisions. Signals help to improve the efficiency of communication between strangers, since they enable both sides to grasp information they care most in face of total unknown. As a result, signals play a key role in selection process, and wherever there is selection, there is the role of signals.

Signals are especially useful for recruiters since they must make important decisions relating to selecting the right candidates quickly. One signal reveals certain piece of information, two signals reveal several pieces of information and by gathering up different signals, recruiters could build up a relatively complete picture of strangers that are applying for positions in his company. This picture may not be comprehensive and accurate but is good enough for deciding whether or not to recruit certain people.

6.4 Signals and youth unemployment

This book tries to understand young people's unemployment by focusing on recruitment, and let's figure out the relationship between signals and youth unemployment.

Two sides of the table in the interview room, recruiters sit on one side and job applicants on the other side. Recruiters, while they possess the authority of deciding whether or not to hire one candidate, they are not supermen and would not state that they could always make the right decisions. They have their advantages and disadvantages, and they perform the roles of recruiters simply because they have such sorts of knowledge and abilities. They are realistic about the fact that recruitment is just one part of their duty, and they have to find ideal candidates for the firm with limited time and budget. And thus, recruiters do not aim at the best or perfect candidate and satisfice is enough.

"Satisfice" used here may be different from the Merriam-Webster definition of satisfice, which is "to pursue the minimum satisfactory condition or outcome"[92], since a minimum satisfactory situation is perhaps as hard to measure as a maximum satisfactory situation. Satisfice is suited to be used here only to remind us the task of recruitment for recruiters: it is not about recruiting the best to achieve a perfect match, but about recruiting people who could fit in the company in an efficient way. They won't scrutinize each material provided by applicants in detail, but will search for favorable signals—after all, their attention will only stay on the resume of one candidate for a short period of time, which would become less if too many candidates are competing for the same position.

When selecting candidates, instead of taking a careful examination of what kind of person the candidate is, recruiters largely base their judgment on signals that the candidate possesses. Thus, to figure out why many youths fail during recruitment is almost equal to figure out why those youth do not possess signals that are welcomed by recruiters or possess signals that are disliked by recruiters.

Now, we could better understand the role of a college degree. College degree is welcomed and considered as a necessary signal for many positions, and we must accept it since companies have the right to make their recruitment requirement. For some companies, a college degree is crucial and without it, they do not want to spend time to explore more about whether one candidate is suited for their firms. On one hand, this is because there were few other methods that could provide a clear description about how competent one candidate is, not to mention the fact that there always existing errors; On the other hand, firms am not motivated to take efforts to understand more about one candidate, since there are other applicants who possess what they need—a college degree. To try to figure out the competences of people is usually time consuming, and companies are not willing to bear risks associated with working with someone unknown.

For recruiters to make their decisions, signals often come first, before trying to understand what kind of person one candidate is. The candidate may be a good guy and always kind to people, but in order to survive in the business world, he must also contribute to the company's business—he must be professional enough. This doesn't necessarily mean recruiters have no interest in understanding what kind of person their candidates are—they definitely do since they are actually hiring their future colleagues with whom they will be working with, rather than some unrelated people. However, it is difficult to know exactly what kind of person one candidate is, and it is generally impossible to make a conclusion since we human beings are complicated. What's more, job seekers may simply lie during recruitment, which makes the question of "what kind of person the candidate is" even more unreliable. This is why signals are extremely important for recruiters.

Different from personalized stuffs, signals such as a college degree, a professional certificate or a recognized-experience are those third-party accreditations that would indicate the ability and experience of people. Since they are often standardized just as a TOEFL score, they are easily understood and are easily used for comparison purpose— especially when we realize that people are quite different from each other. Besides standardization, signals are also widely accepted for their reliability. Questions and structures of a TOEFL test is carefully designed and a college degree means the degree holder has passed all those requirements that are embedded in his learning process. Signals indicate professional abilities and are readily accepted and are easy to use, and this has further stressed the importance of signals. This preference reflected in resume scrutinizing is that recruiters expect their candidates to describe their achievements with more numbers rather than words. Words vary greatly, but numbers are accurate.

We could also understand Recruitment Formula from the perspective of signals. Remember in chapter 4, in order to understand whether young people themselves should also be responsible for their unemployment, I propose a recruitment formula, which could be extended to three aspects: skill-related issue, X-factor and interest-related issue. Based on facts collected, I conclude that many youths are not competent enough for employment, which also means those youths do not possess signals desired by recruiters.

Recruiters try to grasp candidates' signals which could help them figure out whether these candidates meet their recruitment criteria. For example, skill-related issue concerns how skilled the job seeker is, and a high TOEFL score or one year of study in UK would send a signal that the candidate having a good command of English. Similarly, a person used to take part in team sports like football or basketball would be an acceptable signal showing recruiters that the candidate has less problem dealing with teamwork, which partly answers X-factor related concern. And even for interest-related issue, recruiters could also find clues through signals: a good knowledge of the company that he is applying for is a nice signal that he is really interested in the company, and this is also known as a sign of interest.

As a result, young people fail to obtain jobs for not meeting recruitment requirement and this could be understood as they do not possess recognized signals that are welcomed by recruiters. Recruiters look for signals during their recruitment and they will turn down those who do not possess signals they desire or those who possess signals that they dislike. And thus, young people's employment issue is particularly reflected in their possession of signals.

One thing needs to be clarified that I have focused on recruitment to understand the reasons of youth unemployment problem, but this doesn't mean technique skills such as resume writing skills or interview skills are the most important things. While good techniques do help young people behave better during recruitment, the fundamental and crucial things are still their competencies, which are reflected on signals they possess.

6.5 A brief clarification about signals

Signals matter in recruitment because they help to reduce information asymmetry between recruiters and job seekers, and this role is based on three characteristics of signals: significance, standardization and independence.

Significance means signals would send explicit information with certain level of importance. If information indicated is not accurate but ambiguous, it won't contribute to people's decision. Let's use the case of a swimming pool to understand this characteristic.

Before entering the water, people would want to know the depth of the pool, especially for those who are not good at swimming. But if the operator of the swimming pool just tells visitors that the depth of the pool is less than three meters, visitors would get puzzled since they want to know the accurate depth so as to decide whether they could stay there safely. Similarly, it would also be useless if the operator tells visitors that there are stores selling ten kinds of magazines near the swimming pool. While ten is an accurate number, it contributes little to customers' decision of whether bring their children to the swimming pool and thus is considered no importance. Clarity and importance collectively make up the first characteristic of signals: significance.

Standardization is the second characteristic of signals, which means to use standardized and simplified indicators or results to represent quite different as well as complicated things.

In bond market, three credit rating agencies enjoy worldwide reputation—Moody's Investors Service, Standard & Poor's and Fitch Ratings, and all of them only use a few letters to indicate the debt-paying ability of economic entities. For example, in Moody's system, they use nine symbols to reflect creditworthiness— Aaa, Aa, A, Baa, Ba, B, Caa, Ca, and C, and from Aa to Caa they will also add 1, 2, or 3 as modifiers[93]. In this system, securities rated range from Aaa to Baa3 are at investment level and securities with ratings range from Ba1 to C stay at speculative level. Through such symbols, we could easily grasp the creditworthiness of certain entities for evaluation purpose, and this is the second characteristic of signals: standardization. Through standardization, we could understand and compare different entities under a uniform system, and thus is much efficient.

The third characteristic of signals is independence. With significance and standardization, signals help people to form a basic understanding about certain target, but this understanding isn't trustworthy until it is backed up by independence. If signals are not obtained from independent third-party issuers, people would have a reason to doubt about their creditability. If results presented are not trustworthy, they are again useless, and this is why independence is also a crucial characteristic of signals. For example, according to the standards of professional conduct of CFA institute, research analysts are better to refuse compensation that is linked to the results of their research reports, otherwise their independence will be compromised, and their reports become less trustworthy.

Significance, standardization and independence are three characteristics of signals that we are discussing about, and besides these examples given above, there are many other examples in our daily life. In fact, due to the effect of reducing information asymmetry, signals are prevailing in our lives. Tertiary education is an important topic in the discussion of youth unemployment problem, and in USA, the Ivy League consists of eight top schools. Here, "Ivy League" could be considered as a signal for those education providers, since it means high quality and good reputation of its members. Besides, for business schools, there are three accreditations that indicate high quality: AACSB, EQUIS and AMBA, and those having obtained all of these three accreditations are typically referred to as Triple accreditation or Triple Crown accreditation[94], which is definitely a widely-accepted honor.

Signals doesn't exist just in education fields, but everywhere. In the business world, there are rankings such as Fortune Global 500 yearly list, which would be a good signal for those in the list, since it means largest companies in the world. In entertainment industry, there are awards such Academy Award, often referred to as The Oscars, and a movie winning a title in the Oscars ceremony would be a great honor that indicates the quality of that movie. In sports industry, there are rankings of athletes, clubs as well as national teams, and those in the forefront of such lists would be considered as the best in the world. In personal development area, there are endless certificates such as education diplomas, professional certificates like CFA, FRM, and skill certificates like TOEFL, IELTS.

People may lie and make up stories so as to please recruiters, but those external signals are relatively independent and hard to manipulate, and this makes them easier to be accepted by recruiters. This doesn't mean that people's personal experience which are usually not standardized or obtained from the third-party cannot send signals to other people. In fact, personal experience is definitely something that recruiters care about, such as work experience or internship experience, and they will use many different techniques such as asking detailed questions to verify the reliability of such experience. Besides recognized experience, people's personal stories could also send signals, but these stories are hard to verify and thus usually play a less important role than those third-party signals that are recognized by the general public. Here I mean, signal is a broad concept that does not only include standardized things such as certificates or diplomas, but also include non-standardized experience that is significant and could be verified.

There is sort of continuity for people's abilities, which means what happened in the past tends to repeat in the future, and thus through the set of signals that one candidate possesses, recruiters can form an idea concerning what they could expect from this candidate. However, just like food and drinks, which have expiration date, there is period of validity for many signals: for example, TOEFL score validates within only two years. This means if some youths want to exhibit such signals to recruiters, they must pay attention to the time that they are expected to obtain such signals, otherwise their hard work of obtaining such signals may not contribute for their seeking employment.

However, period of validity is in fact less of a concern when it is compared to the fact that there are so many kinds of signals, and different companies will look for different signals from their candidates. This means that we could not answer whether one signal is important or not, and thus just possessing some good signals is not enough, young people have to possess the RIGHT ones.

6.6 The formation of signals

The key to have a job is to pass recruitment, which requires the possession of certain signals, including but not limited to standard certificates and recognized experience. But for many youths, only when they enter job market to seek employment would they realize their lack of such signals, and thus fail to pass recruitment. However, at that time, those youths can do nothing to alter their situation even if they have known what signals employers are looking for: it's just too late to make any changes concerning signals they possess, and they have to accept their difficulty of seeking employment. Most signals are not formed within a short period of time, just as *Rome wasn't built in a day*. What signals indicate is years of accumulation and preparation.

In normal cases, as children grow up, they will become more experienced and have accomplished many achievements, all of which will turn into their competitive advantages that are sensed and grasped by recruiters as signals. Some people will accumulate more signals (including skills formed, which could be sensed by recruiters during interviews) and others will accumulate less, and this will affect their career prospect. The question that why many youths fail to obtain jobs due to the lack of competencies is almost equal to ask why those youths are short of signals that are favored by employers when they seek employment. And when we move a step forward, this question is further equal to ask why those youths do not obtain those signals before they enter job market. The specific time of obtaining those signals or forming certain skills may vary, they share a same feature: obtained before the youth entering job market.

Signals being examined during recruitment are not formed and obtained during the interview, but much earlier before the interview takes place. A key standard signal, education diploma, is obtained in each periods of children's growing process. And for non-standard signals such as relevant skills, internship experience or signs of interest towards a company, due to their difficulty and complexity, the result of having such signals equally mean that those candidates are on the road to obtain these signals long before they enter job market.

Signals are closely related to time.

On one hand, the obtaining of certain signals is generally possible within a specific time period, which means once this time period has passed by, people wouldn't be able to gain those signals, and chances may fade away. Let's again still use the case of a university diploma to understand this.

In most cases, the time that people pursue their university study will be shortly after their graduating from high school, and once they miss this chance, their opportunities to go on their university study will fall gradually or become too difficult to be considered as realistic for the general public. This is mainly due to the fact that as people become older, they are faced with more tasks, such as making money to stand on their own feet, getting married, raising children and so on. All those things will bring extra burden, take up their time and make them harder to be concentrated. As a result, even if universities are usually open for people at all ages, the older have more difficulties than the youth to pursue further study.

On the other hand, signals are just indicators of competencies and skills, and the formation of competencies as well as skills relate not only to time, but also to abilities. In many cases, people have to form signals gradually, which means they must also "learn to walk before running".

For any specific area, there is typically a series of signals, and there is kind of progressive relationship between these signals: one can only obtain lower ones before they are qualified to earn upper ones. Education process is such an example, that we will typically finish primary school, middle school and high school one by one, and only after high school will comes university study. For standard signals such as CFA certificate, there are three levels, and before earning the designation, one has to pass the tests of all three levels one by one, which might take more than 2 years. For non-standard signals like internship experience, people have to start from the most basic task, like printing files, and then undertake more responsibility as they become more experienced and better familiar with work environment.

Signals are just indicators of people's skills, and people's skills can only progress step by step through the time. This is the thing that makes a difference for young people: during recruitment, while young people realize what signals they need, they are just unable to gain these signals immediately.

To conclude, what signals reflect is the accumulation of achievements through years, a situation that won't change much overnight. Many people may need to improve their skills concerning writing resumes or taking part in interviews, and sometimes improvement in these areas do help them get their desired jobs, but this doesn't change the statement that what will be examined during recruitment are signals, since while how to write resume properly could be mastered quickly, the contents of one's resume would only form gradually, and while what would be discussed during an interview may be learned quickly, the stories within discussions as well as the confidence during such conversations can only derive from past experience.

In short, signals that recruiters emphasize on during recruitment are just indicators of candidates' consecutive preparation and accumulation.

6.7 The logic of youth unemployment problem

This book has taken the perspective of labor supply to understand the causes of youth unemployment crisis, and to be specific, the focus is why many youths fail to meet the requirements of employers, which are reflected in the components of Recruitment Formula.

But this is not the whole story on labor-supply aspect, since many youths may simply turn down jobs that they consider as below their expectations and ambitions. The situation of working poverty as mentioned in section 5.9 has made young people's rejecting low-paid jobs an apprehensible choice. However, if those who reject low-paid jobs could also apply for better ones, and then we have to ask why they do not receive offers from those better jobs. As a result, our analysis up to now would also cover this group of youths and based on one key assumption of this book that there are significant number of job opportunities available to the youth, we could state that our analysis could reflect the whole story on labor-supply side.

As mentioned before, when youths grow up, they will become more experienced and have accumulated competencies, which would be sensed by recruiters as signals. Young people fail to obtain jobs because they could not provide enough signals that are required by recruiters, and they cannot alter this situation since the formation as well as accumulation of signals is a long process, not only for standard signals such as certificates or diplomas, but also for non-standard signals like internship experience or skills.

As a result, rescue mechanisms aiming at providing more apprenticeships and permanent jobs may not operate well as are expected. These mechanisms ask companies to recruit more youths, without figuring out whether those youths are competent enough for those jobs or really interested in those companies, and thus companies cannot help doubting about whether those newly recruited youths are really suited for their companies or would they leave quickly after getting trained. Under a situation like this, companies are not willing to invest much in those youths or let them assume more responsibility and must rely on external funds such as support from governments to arrange those apprenticeship programs.

The role of signals during recruitment is quite similar to that of paper currency during transactions, and one basic principle of transactions is that the delivery of goods gets along with payment. When young people do not provide signals required by employers, employers are not willing to recruit them or will not invest too much in their development. As such, to ask companies to recruit more is one sort of government intervention in economy that may have negative side effects, in which case neither companies nor governments are satisfied, and also those youths since if they can only get access to basic tasks during their training programs, their skills won't grow, especially from a long-term perspective.

When we are trying to tackle youth unemployment problem, if our attention just focuses on the time point that the youth enter job market, we may miss the point. While crisis occurs at this period of time, those actual problems might lie in the growing process of the youth. There will be unprepared youths coming into job market in the future, and we are not sure whether the society then could also provide more training positions for them, especially when macroeconomic conditions are not good.

For many young people, there exists disparity between their expectations and the reality, which happens as a result of lacking acknowledgement about their own skills and interests, about situations in job markets and about specific requirements concerning their desired jobs. This relates to not only information, but also wealth, and the youth must have wealth to support their personal development. As have been stressed in chapter 5 that for young people, wealth and information largely come from family members, those grow up in poor background will suffer more from youth unemployment problem, and thus we could say that youth unemployment crisis occurs as a part of wealth inequality problem.

Now we have completed the logic of labor-supply analysis about the causes of youth unemployment problem: young people fail to get employment because they do not possess signals required by employers, a result of their inadequate preparation and reflects the disparity between their expectations and the realities. This disparity exists further as a result of lacking information and wealth in those youths' growing process. For the youth, information and wealth mainly come from their families and thus, young people are unemployed because their families could not provide them with enough information and wealth—since there is kind of consistence between the possession of wealth and the possession of information, we could say that youth unemployment happens as a result of wealth inequality. The formation of skills and the accumulation of experience need time, and those youth will not be able to gather up enough signals at the time they seek employment, even if they have realized their unpreparedness, and this is why methods focusing on creating more job positions are not considered as sustainable, especially from a long-term point of view.

As a result, the key to conquer youth unemployment problem from a long-term point of view, is to provide the future generations with adequate support concerning wealth as well as information, so as to help them better prepare for employment—long before they enter job market to seek employment.

6.8 One serious yet neglected social problem

Following the elaboration of signals, one serious yet neglected problem—compared to youth unemployment crisis—emerges, and this section aims to reveal it to readers. But firstly, let's review the discussion about "signals".

In chapter six, my analysis is conducted based on the discussion of signals, which is not only easy to understand but also easy to arouse misunderstandings. Due to thought inertia, "signals" used here is easy to get mixed with other descriptions such as "qualifications". In other words, for readers, it is easy to think signals that employers expect during their recruitment refer to something that is specific and concrete, like diplomas or certificates. And qualifications have been used in many places to explain the reasons of unemployment, such as one figure in professor Vogel's *Generation Jobless? Turning the Youth Unemployment Crisis into Opportunity* which shows reasons for not getting a job: based on the data of FutureWork Forum(2010) [95], it states that "insufficient qualifications" accounts for around 17% failure of seeking employment, which stands as one reason along with "lack of experience", "other" and etc.

However, signals in my book cannot be considered as equal to qualifications or certificates, even though they share many similarities. Here I use signals in my book because this description reflects the core problem of recruitment that due to information asymmetry, employers need credible messages to aid them in their hiring decision—and I refer to such messages as signals. In section 6.5, I have mentioned that there are standard signals and non-standard signals, and only the standard group of signals could be considered as things like qualifications.

Once we realize that signals and qualifications are not exactly the same thing, we would easily notice one key difference between them: the possession of qualifications is always a positive thing, but the possession of signals might be positive or negative. To understand this, let's consider qualifications as gold, and to have gold will always means some fortune; but to consider signals as traffic lights, that we can pass only when the green light is on, and when the red light is on, we can only stop. The thing is, to possess qualifications would always add points for job seekers during recruitment, but the possession of signals could either add points or deduct points.

Before this section, signals discussed in this chapter are mainly positive ones—those desired by employers and thus could add points. But there are also "negative ones", which are rejected by employers and would deduct points for job seekers. During recruitment, recruiters would also care about negative signals, and sometimes, the existence of negative signals may perform a role like veto, which could ruin all the hard work and efforts of a job seeker. In some cultures, severe criminal records may occasionally play such a role, and when applying for a teach position in top universities, a lack of doctoral degree might also lead to the veto effect. One thing needs to be mentioned that this veto effect of negative signals has nothing to do with employment discrimination, with the latter violating people's rights while veto effect of negative signals deriving from the needs of certain job positions.

Compared with the impact of negative signals, the formation of such signals is extremely easy, which doesn't need long period of accumulation as is expected in the formation of positive ones. Recall the words of Warren Buffet, that "It takes 20 years to build a reputation and 5 minutes to ruin it. If you think about that, you'll do things differently." His words reveal the difference between the formation of positive signals and negative ones, and the latter part of his words is exactly what young people should bear in mind, especially when they are dealing with important things such as seeking employment—they should pay attention to accumulate positive signals and avoid negative ones.

Long period of unemployment may turn into negative signals under certain conditions. In the latest youth unemployment crisis, we know that many youths turn down entry-level jobs and they have every reason to do this, such as the fear of working poverty. But this is not ideal from the perspective of signals, since long-term unemployment may become a negative signal in these people's future attempts of seeking employment. In the very beginning of this book, I have introduced studies showing that those who have experienced unemployment in the start stage of their career tend to have more problems concerning employment as they become older, with a higher risk compared to other people to fall into long-term unemployment. This higher risk of long-term unemployment could be understood from the less accumulation of skills, which reflects a lack of positive signals, or equally, a possession of negative signals.

In December of 2017, The Economists issued a brochure titled *10 Things We Learned in 2017*[96], in which one thing is referred to as why the world's most valuable resource is now data, not oil. This is not an anticipation of the future, but a description of current trend, that the era of big data has come. In the era of big data, data will be collected frequently and used widely—abide by the law of course, which might cause disadvantages for those who have many negative signals, since such signals would become more prominent than before. And thus, to accept basic jobs during economic downturn becomes a wise choice, since this avoids the likely negative implication of unemployment as signals. Otherwise, as the period of unemployment extends, it may cause those youths dropping out of labor force.

Our society operates following many rules and only those who cater for those rules would succeed more easily. Due to information asymmetry, one basic principle is to avoid the accumulation of negative signals, and this has revealed the serious yet neglected problem: the accumulation of negative signals may cause too many young people to drop out of labor force, which may prevent them from fully participating in normal life and make it difficult from them to become independent. In other words, youth unemployment problem may turn into social exclusion problem, and as this group enlarges, it may become a black swan event for the society.

Readers may question that it is not sufficient to understand labor-supply side reasons of youth unemployment just from recruitment, since young people could set up their own businesses, and thus wouldn't need other people to hire them. This is a reasonable question, and many researchers have also called for entrepreneurship to tackle youth unemployment. However, to set up one's own business, there is a need of technical skills, management talents, work experience as well as initial funds, which are typically not realistic for young people.

Generally speaking, those who could set up their own businesses could also work for others, yet those who could work for others may not be able to establish their own businesses, and this is especially true for young people who just step out of school. If, as has been illustrated in the former part of this book, that many youths are not competent enough for getting a job, we couldn't count on their entrepreneurship. Most youths are expected to work for other people for certain periods, after which could they consider set up their own businesses, and as a result, highlighting entrepreneurship should not be treated as a major solution of tackling youth unemployment problem. In fact, I believe it is those current entrepreneurs who should highlight entrepreneurship, since they are more experienced and have many resources, and when they take steps to expand their businesses, they will hire more youths, which would contribute to the mitigation of youth unemployment crisis.

In my analysis of recruitment, the thing that is reflected by the benefit-cost analysis and the extended three aspects—skill-related issue, X-factor and interest-related issue, is not just the need of employers, but also the requirement of job market and future competitions. As a result, simple as it is, the focus of recruitment is relatively comprehensive and complete. And from the perspective of young people, the word that's addressed extensively in this chapter, signal, does not equal to something concrete, but more like a sort of awareness that they should pay attention to accumulate their competitive advantages and their selling points—things that could be received by employers as positive signals, and avoid the accumulation of negative signals. They should be aware that their choices made today could affect their future, and thus to be more cautious when they make important decisions.

Information asymmetry, signals and the dimension of time

Part C: The solution of youth unemployment problem

7. INFORMATION EQUALITY IS THE KEY

7.1 Elaboration of solutions

Finally, it comes to the stage of discussing solutions of youth unemployment problem. But firstly, l would like to reiterate the focus of this book, and I will do this by starting with an example from sports.

We know many top teams stopped at the group stage during their 2014 World Cup journey, and this was a problem for many countries at that time. When people notice this issue, what they can do is not encouraging them to move a step further in 2014 World Cup, but to encourage them to perform better in the next one—in the future. Similarly, the focus concerning youth unemployment problem in this book, is not today's unemployed youths or current youth unemployment situation, but youths in the future, and aims to prevent youth unemployment crisis from reoccurring in the future. Existing researches, discussions as well as policies have been exhaustively focused on current situation and today's youths, and my analysis from a different standpoint will enrich our understanding about youth unemployment problem.

Based on discussions in the former part of this book, we know that many youths do not prepare well for employment, both mentally and technically, which happens as a result of lacking wealth and information. Employers need signals to assist them make decisions, but many youths do not provide enough signals, and this is a situation that cannot revert right now since the formation of signals requires time. As a result, the solution of preventing youth unemployment crisis from recurring in the future is to provide adequate wealth as well as information to the future generations during their growing process, so as to help them prepare well for employment.

Wealth is relatively difficult to provide, since it couldn't be copied. Just contrary to wealth, information could be shared and is easily spread among the public with little cost, and the solution proposed in my book will emphasize on the aspect of information, summarized as promoting the equality of information.

7.2 The role of information

Everyone knows that information is very important and matters everywhere, but few have realized how important it is on youth unemployment issue.

Let's first have a look at this question: who is more likely to carry on when they are faced with great difficulty during a task, the one who is confident about himself or the one who believes his effort will pay off? When we get this question, the first thought would be that the one with courage will more likely to go on, simply because people can do nothing without courage. But does this explanation credible?

Largely not, since in reality we won't do anything that we could do, and this is because we have limited time or energy. Even if a man is confident about his ability, before determined to move on, he still has to ask him questions like whether he could finish the task, or what's the price of doing that and what's the payoff. Few people would do something that they would not benefit from—unless those derived from their sincere interest, in which case doing itself is the benefit, and thus if they believe they could benefit from what they do, or they know that their efforts will pay off, they will be more likely to carry on.

In fact, we could find similar result in cases relating to business management.

At the stage of evaluating a new investment, companies will typically perform a NPV analysis that calculates the net present value of an investment. And only if the NPV of the investment were significantly larger than zero, would the company have an interest to move forward. Here, in the firm's decision about an investment, there is no factor concerning whether the firm's CEO is confident or not, but a factor concerning whether the investment will be expected to bring positive return for the firm—when we apply this thought to understand the question that we've proposed in the start of this section, firm's concern about the NPV of an investment is just like a person's concern about whether his efforts will pay off. Only when the NPV of an investment is significantly larger than zero would the firm have an interest to go into the investment, and for a person, only if he believes his effort will pay off, he will carry on.

When it comes to doing something difficult, whether one is confident or not, or whether he could do it or not isn't that important, since a person could do many things. The thing that determines his doing that task, is the acknowledgment that his efforts will pay off. And how could people know whether or not their efforts will pay off in the future? This is where information helps. The key value of information is that it encourages people to adjust their behaviors now so as to have a favorable result in the future.

Remember in MCG's report, there is one category of youths that called "too cool to pursue tertiary education". The moment I read this I cannot help wondering whether it is reasonable to set up such a category. This is because for a rational person, under the assumption that he could afford the cost of tertiary education, he would go on his study, since based on our former discussions, such an advanced degree will bring positive NPV later during his life. I've been wondering whether those who are clarified as "to cool to go on" would change their minds if they possess the information relating to the positive value of tertiary education. This is important, since if the answer of no interest in post-secondary education derives not from their choice, but from their lack of relevant information, we must let them know such information.

Come back to the question that I proposed in the beginning of this section: who are more likely to move on? The one who knows his effort will pay off. And the "knows" here relates to one thing: information.

7.3 The interaction between information and wealth

Remember in section 5.7, I have discussed the consistency between information and wealth, which means wealthier people tend to get access to better information, and I illustrate this by using "employment" as the bridge that links wealth and information. Here in this section, I will not repeat the consistency between them, instead I will discuss the interaction between them.

It is widely accepted that education experience will help young people to get a job and generally, as education level rises, youth unemployment rate falls. This means those who step into job market with a primary or below-secondary education experience suffer more from youth unemployment crisis. This is not difficult to understand. For those who enter job market shortly after finishing primary school, there is an obvious disadvantage that they are short of work experience or even internship experience. At a young age, they are generally too young to take up any internships, not to mention that there are laws prohibiting child labor.

To enter job market at a young age tends to be less experienced, but is this for sure? Certainly not. When we read stories of successful people, we notice that many of them did some basic work such as delivering newspaper at a young age, as was required by their parents, so as to develop their communication skills and the sense of duty in workplace. This method helps, while the task of delivering newspaper is relatively simple, it does help children to develop their skills and their sense of duty.[i] Here in this case, thanks to their parents' requesting them to deliver newspaper, children could still develop their skills even at a young age. I would say that this relates to information, since only when those children's parents know the value of such experience, would they ask their children to do that: this knowledge is information.

Suppose those youths who are supposed to enter job market without a college degree obtain such information that they need some work experience to get a job, would they choose to conduct some simple jobs or similar tasks during the leisure time of their study? Even though more experience won't guarantee their employment, it would definitely provide them with more opportunities and thus increases their chances of getting a good job. When they have jobs, they could start from the bottom and make progress gradually, through which process they would become more and more competent, and finally, the disadvantages led by not participating in higher levels of education may get offset.

We already know that cost, or wealth, is the main reason for young people's giving up education and entering job market at a young age. From the case above we find that, the possession of information would help those youths better prepare for their employment and may even reverse the disadvantages caused by not possessing a college degree. This means, the possession of information could alter the disadvantages led by lacking wealth, or in other words, the possession of information alters the situation about wealth.

Let's have a look at another case that the possession of information alters the situation about wealth, and this case is also about education.

It is widely recognized that lacking wealth has prevented many youths from pursuing a university degree, but there are also large number of people who cannot afford the cost of tertiary education yet have finished their studies successfully—with the help of scholarships or student loans. This help is closely related to information, since only if those students know there exist such aids would they apply for them, and if they could not get access to information about such aids, they wouldn't get this help.

---

[i] Of course, safety issues should be stressed for children performing tasks like this

Besides, it is not enough to simply know the existence of such aids, they should also know the requirements of such scholarships or loans, and the early the better. This is because these aids are not available for all those who need them. Competition is high and only those who meet their criteria would obtain such aids. If a young person growing up from poor background realizes the existence of such aids and their corresponding requirements, he is likely to try his best to prepare himself well for obtaining such aids, such as getting higher grades in his study. For some people, they would successfully obtain those aids and finish their study in university, and once again, the possession of information alters the disadvantaged situation brought by lacking wealth.

In fact, not only the possession of information could alter the situation about wealth, the possession of wealth could also alter the situation about information. And this is much easier to understand, since people could buy services to let them know more about education, employment and other important issues.

For example, by paying charges, people could have their own tutors, take many personality tests, and take part in more social activities. Home tutors could help young people to gain knowledge about certain areas; personality tests, while their imperfection, could help test-takers understand more about themselves; and abundant experience in social activities could help young people know more about how to behave in different occasions, and thus would help them to fit in different environment. If the knowledge mentioned here are considered as certain types of information, we could state that the possession of wealth alters the situation about information.

We know that wealth plays a role in youth unemployment issue, and so does information. However, the impact of wealth and information towards young people's employment is not that simple as "1+1=2"—wealth and information do not work separately, but more like a cup of Café au Lait: in the bottle there exists both coffee and milk, and when one drinks it, the taste he feels is not coffee or milk but coffee with milk, since the existence of milk has changed the taste of coffee and the existence of coffee has also changed the taste of milk.

In the growing process of young people, there is interaction between wealth and information: wealth does not only have an impact over the growing of youth, but also has an influence over the information that they obtain, and information does not only make a difference in young people's growing, but also alters the status of wealth that the youth possess, or wealth that young people could get access to, and finally, it is wealth and information collectively, that have an impact over young people's growing process. As a result, concerning youth unemployment problem, the internal mechanism is the interaction between wealth and information, as well as their collective influence over young people.

The interaction between information and wealth, or in other words, the fact that the possession of information could alter the situation concerning wealth, provides us a clue to understand the formation and solution of youth unemployment problem. We all know that the lack of wealth is hard to change, but what about the lack of information? If we could provide adequate information, through the interaction between information and wealth and their joint influence over young people, we may have a chance to conquer youth unemployment problem, especially for the poor.

7.4 The inequality of information

It is well known that there exists inequality of wealth in our human society, but there also exists the inequality of information, which has largely been neglected. My focus in this section, is the inequality of information.

One source of information is experience, and there is an obvious difference between the information possessed by those who have jobs and those who don't. The difference of information is also prevailing among those who have jobs—as long as there is difference between personal experience, there is difference concerning information. For example, a professional basketball player and a mathematics teacher hold different set of knowledge, or information, and so do for a basketball player and a football player, or that between a mathematics teacher and a history teacher.

Employment in different industries, such as the former case concerning a teacher and an athlete, typically equip people with different sets of skills, and the knowledge about these skills as well as the information concerning how to develop those skills are valuable. Even for those who work in the same industry, their knowledge bases are different since there are different business functions and different job types. What's more, for those who work in the same business function and department, there exists diversity of information. People from higher levels are in charge of more things, taking greater responsibilities, dealing with more people and participating in more activities, which means naturally, those who hold a higher position possess more information compared with their subordinates.

Besides personal experience, people could also get information from what they read, such as books, newspapers, websites, and what they discuss about during chatting with relatives and friends. These latter two channels are especially important for young people, since they have little personal experience concerning employment, and must rely on external sources to absorb information.

Experience, books and other people are just sources of information, and the varied ability to interpret and utilize information would also contribute to the difference of information among people. After all, the value of information only comes true when people have taken actions utilizing it, and if people do not know how to utilize it or to utilize it in a wrong way, to possess more information won't help much.

What's more, all that has been discussed above is just the difference concerning information from the perspective of quantity, which refers to how much information people have, but contrary to the possession of wealth, to possess a large quantity of information is not always a good thing. Compared with quantity, this is another perspective concerning the quality of information, which could be referred to as how helpful information is for people.

Readers could understand the difference between the quantity of information and the quality of information through a comparison between reserve currencies such as dollars or euros, and the local currencies of some developing countries. From the perspective of quantity, the more the better is suited for both reserve currencies and local currencies, but from the perspective of quality, a smaller amount of reserve currencies may be better than a large quantity of local currencies, since the value of reserve currencies are relatively stable, yet local currencies are more likely to experience hyperinflation—in which case their values will drop suddenly and dramatically.

In fact, information overload nowadays has become an issue for our society and it is the quality of information that actually matters more. All those factors discussed above have caused the difference concerning information possessed by people, and when this difference leads people to make different decisions on important issues in their lives, it turns into information inequality. Information inequality would have an impact over the quality as well as effectiveness of decisions made by people, which would then affect the competencies and employment of these people.

Youth unemployment rate rises this time because many youths do not prepare well for employment, both mentally and technically, and this happens partly for their lack of understanding about themselves and acknowledgement about situations on job market. The value of information is closely related to time and even if young people have obtained one piece of valuable information, they may still be unable to benefit from it since the value of this piece of information for them has worn off as time passes. For young people, the crucial issue is that they must have adequate information during their growing up, and for youth unemployment problem, the real problem is information inequality before young people entering job market to seek employment.

However, just contrary to the hot discussion about wealth inequality, there is little attention being paid to the inequality of information. This is partly because compared with wealth, information is less concrete and definite, could hardly be measured and people cannot really touch information as they do when they are holding gifts that they have just bought using money. To possess certain amount of wealth would make people happy since it could instantly fulfill their needs, such as through shopping or eating, whereas the possession of information wouldn't grasp the attention of people since the impact of information is less direct, less certain and usually takes more time.

Even so, the inequality of information is still an important issue, especially in the discussion of youth unemployment problem.

7.5 The transferability of information

From the perspective of labor supply and under the assumption of sufficient job opportunities, youth unemployment problem occurs as part of wealth inequality and information inequality. Wealth inequality is hard to change and what about information inequality? If we could promote information equality, we could then reduce wealth inequality through the interaction between information and wealth, and thus conquer youth unemployment from a long-term point of view. Luckily, information inequality is not as stubborn as the inequality of wealth, which could be understood from the following three aspects.

Before moving on, I need to reiterate that information discussed in this book mainly concerns employment, which is public or not difficult to obtain, and thus it has nothing to do with business secrets or scientific insights, which are often not ready-made and require long period of investigation. In a word, information discussed in this book could be considered as a type of existence, and it's just that those who need it do not have it.

Not let's have a look at three characteristics of information, which declare its differences with wealth and indicate its core feature: transferability.

Firstly, there are more sources of information.

Wealth inequality is hard to solve partly due to the fact that there are only a few sources of wealth, which typically include two: inheriting from family members and earn by oneself—through work. Inheriting a big fortune is not realistic for most people and to make a big fortune through employment relies highly on skills of the person, which would make it impossible for everyone. While there are welfare system and fiscal transfer payment, the amount of wealth that transfers through these channels to citizens is limited and thus won't be considered as an effective way to accumulate wealth.

Contrary to wealth, the sources of information are not a few, but a lot. At the very beginning of human society, information was closely attached to personal experience, and knowledge came from the experience of his own. Later, as language appeared and through talking to each other, people could get information from other people, which indicated the partly dissociation of information from people's own experience. Gradually, as paper was created, people could get information through reading and the result was that one's source of information was not limited to people. This phenomenon has been reinforced nowadays, with the help of multimedia and Internet. And through paper, electronic devices and the Internet, information could get spread without the constraints of time and space, and now we know that there are so many sources of information that everyone could get access to.

This judgment doesn't conflict with my former statement that for young people, information concerning employment mainly comes from family members, since at the time they need such information, they are too young to realize such needs, but must rely on other people.

Secondly, information could be reproduced endlessly.

For an individual person, the creation and accumulation of wealth is not easy, which is often associated with huge cost, risk and is often time-consuming. But there is no such concern for information. One person knows one piece of information while the other one doesn't, both of them will know this piece of information when one talks to the other. If so, two people know this piece of information, and information is thus doubled. In fact, information could get reproduced by writing down on papers, putting on blogs, or simply talking to someone…it is not difficult at all to reproduce information.

For an ounce of gold, one copy of it is still one ounce of gold, and for one piece of information relating to employment, once copy of it may still benefit another youth equally. But when this piece of information is produced continuously, and everybody knows it, would its value drop to zero and end up with being useless? If so, my suggestion of promoting information equality would be meaningless.

I would say this won't constitute a problem, and to promote information equality would definitely benefit the society. As will be illustrated in the next chapter, information covered in promoting information equality mainly consists of certain rules and some public information, and we must accept the fact that we cannot guarantee the success of young people by simply sharing information—their successes are determined by various factors. To promote information equality will let young people know something they should know, so as to help them better prepare for their careers, yet this won't guarantee their successes. As a result, our reproduction of information won't make this piece of information useless.

Thirdly, information is easy to get spread.

We are now at the era of information, and the transfer of information has never been more convenient. Spread here does not only mean the speed of transfer, but also mean reproduction, which implies the sharing of information to other people won't deprive the original person of utilizing the information. This is different from wealth, since even though wealth is easy to transfer with the help of electronic banking, no one would readily transfer their wealth to other people, in which case they will lose the control of their wealth. Information could be easily transferred from one person to another, with the former person suffering no obvious loss, and this is the meaning of spread.

Compared with wealth, information has more sources, could be reproduced endlessly and gets spread easily, and these characteristics mean that the inequality of information is not as stubborn as that of wealth. This transferability of information provides us with a clue to change the inequality of information, and through the interaction between information and wealth, those children who are short of wealth may also prepare well for their employment in the future.

7.6 Three questions about promoting information equality

While the equality of information is theoretically feasible, there are still many things to consider before actions, among which the three listed below are of great importance.

Firstly, what does "equality of information" mean?

As will be discussed in next chapter, information used here refers to some basic rules of life and the knowledge about employment and job market, which won't cover everything. And the equality of information doesn't mean everyone has same information but means to help those who are lack of information know what they should know. As a result, to promote information equality doesn't affect those who have adequate information, but to provide information to those who are in need, and there is no comparison between the quality or quantity of information possessed among people.

The goal of promoting information equality is to let those who are short of information understand more about situations on job market, to adjust their expectations to fit into realities of life, so as to encourage those youths to adjust their behaviors to better prepare for employment. If they know what the reality is and have prepared for it, they won't become panic as many youths did when they enter job market.

Secondly, does the fact that there exists information inequality means those who are short of information have little information from a quantity perspective?

No, it is not. There exists information inequality does not necessarily mean many people have less amount of information, but mainly refers to their lack of relevant information, the quality of their possessed information, and a lack of guidance about how to interpret information effectively.

Information has flooded nowadays, and everyone has to handle large amount of information which may be both inefficient and exhausting. Meantime, this flood of unrelated information has consolidated the inequality of information, since time is limited, 24 hours a day, and spending too much time dealing with unrelated information will leave less time analyzing useful information. What's worse, the flood of unrelated information may prevent people from getting access to useful information, and this happens when people's attention focuses too much on things unrelated to their goals.

The fact that there exists a flood of information has roused the need to select qualified information to communicate to those who need information. Many youths are not short of information, but short of information relevant to their careers, and thus there should be a place for them to obtain information. Meantime, this place should be an authorized one, which matters not only for the quality of information provided, but also for the acceptability of young people. Young people won't trust any information being provided unless it is provided within an authorized place by reliable people.

Thirdly, just adequate information, or relevant information, is enough?

No, just information is not enough.

The philosophy of my analysis doesn't lead to a dramatic or through change to our current systems, like the suggestion of revising education systems, but to propose additional measures to our current systems so as to achieve the goal of helping young people yet having limited influence over other people. Besides, just having relevant information isn't enough too, since the ability to cope with information varies among people, and when possess the same piece of information, people may interpret differently and then act differently. This issue has made the achieving of information equality less helpful, and there should also be mechanisms that could bring the power of information into effect, which means to help young people understand information better, and to encourage young people to alter their behavior accordingly.

No one should take it for granted for having a good job, and people should expect to work hard for what they want. Those who possess adequate information tend to make better choices during their growing up, while those who don't have adequate information are easy to get lost on the road towards proper employment.

8. THE INFORMATION NEEDED

8.1 A multi-stakeholder issue in nature

No stakeholders in youth unemployment issue are satisfied with current situation and based on discussions in the former part of this book, we understand better about why they feel unsatisfied and uncomfortable.

Companies are unsatisfied, since young applicants do not possess signals that they need and thus they cannot tell whether or not those youths are suited for their companies. When required by government to recruit more, they cannot help wondering whether those youths will quit shortly after getting trained and how much they should invest in those youths. And they are uncomfortable simply because they don't know their candidates.

Young people are uncomfortable, since apprenticeship opportunities provided by companies are generally restricted to some basic ones, which do not suit their interests or do not provide a long-term vision, and thus they may not truly benefit from these trainings or apprenticeships. What's more, the formation of signals requires time, and this has reduced their chances of entering their desired firms or industries.

Governments or policy makers are uncomfortable, since those apprenticeship programs rely heavily on funds from government, yet government funds are limited and cannot last long for helping the unemployed youth. Besides, the effects of these apprenticeships remain unclear and many youths have given up midway. Government debt has been rising and so does budgetary deficit, and thus policy makers worry about whether they still have the ability to help the unemployed youths.

So are education institutions, the society as a whole, and other stakeholders.

Even if those stakeholders are unsatisfied and feel uncomfortable, they still have to move on, to work together to help conquer this youth unemployment crisis, since this is the kind of issue that we can't afford to lose. To analyze youth unemployment problem, I have focused on competencies of young people, but it doesn't mean that this problem has nothing to do with other stakeholders, since youth unemployment problem is by its nature a multi-stakeholder issue. Up to now, I have intentionally neglected other stakeholders because I want to reduce the impact on them, which would make any rescue plans more feasible.

Recall the case in section 3.5 about air-conditioner in the classroom, that the setting of temperature of the air-conditioner may be lowered only when the new comers have taken off their overcoat, since this problem is caused by them, and they should first try their best to fit in before asking other people to adjust for them. And for the analysis of youth unemployment problem, I have taken the perspective of labor supply, and analyze it under the assumption that there are adequate job opportunities. This means youth unemployment problem occurs mainly for the reason of the youth. As a result, I have tried to find out how should young people better prepare for their employment before asking other stakeholders to contribute to the tackling of youth unemployment problem.

This doesn't mean that other stakeholders do not need to take actions to cope with youth unemployment problem. Actually, they must do something, but their actions should not be too big but follow an approach similar to KAIZEN[97], a Japanese management philosophy which means continuously improvement for better. What other stakeholders should carry out are not drastic changes but small changes step by step, and this would reduce the risk of doing wrong things since how much they should change for the youth and whether these changes are indeed helpful may only become clear decades later. As a result, for other stakeholders, only if they make small changes step by step would there exists a chance of achieving Pareto Improvement, which means to help the unemployed youth without damaging the benefits of other people.

Right now, I've suggested promoting information equality among young people, and it is time to encourage other stakeholders take actions. But before that, let's have a look at the information that they need to help the youth.

8.2 Who also need information

I have suggested to promote information equality, and besides the youth, who also need the support of information?

When I propose this question, I actually mean which stakeholders should also take part in and contribute to the tackling of youth unemployment problem, since there is no need to bother to provide them with information. But why wouldn't I just change the title of this section and rename it as "Who should also contribute to the tacking of youth unemployment problem"?

Other stakeholders must get involved in since youth unemployment problem is by its nature a multi-stakeholder issue, but I don't want to use such an affirmative tone and urge other stakeholders to do something, in which case they may overact. And I have used current title because it is consistent with the philosophy of this book that emphasizes on the young people themselves to understand youth unemployment and consider youth unemployment problem as the problem of young people rather than problem of other stakeholders. As a result, I introduce them under the framework of promoting information equality and state "who also need information", which would help us better clarify their roles: on one hand they must take part in, since youth unemployment issue matters to all; on the other hand, we cannot expect too much from them, since youth unemployment problem is mainly a problem of young people themselves.

Now, let's see who also need information in the action of promoting information equality.

Firstly, parents.

Based on discussions in chapter 6, we know that it is late for young people to realize their lack of competences when they are seeking employment, since the formation of skills requires time. And correspondingly, we need to provide them with information before they seek employment, when they are quite young. However, children's attention focuses on how to play well, and few of them know they need to work in the future or to prepare carefully for employment. As a result, information provided to children are actually provided to their parents, and only when children have grown up would they be willing to and be able to seek information concerning employment. When people are young, it is their parents' responsibility to take care of them, and thus parents need information.

Secondly, education providers.

Education providers have been extensively mentioned in youth unemployment crisis this time.

The information needed

For most people, when they are young they will stay at home being taken care of by parents or other family members, and then go to school to receive education as they grow older, and only when they have finished several years of education would they enter job market to seek employment. As a result, no matter whether or not education providers, especially those academic programs would like to admit, one of their key roles is to help their students to get employment.

To have a good job is crucial for the welfare of young people, and if this is not stressed during their education process, why would they spend so much time at school? Education providers must get involved in and they need information too.

Thirdly, governments.

The influence of governments is everywhere, and they do need information about how to help young people.

Different from other stakeholders, information provided to policy makers may not contribute to the tackling of youth unemployment problem directly but will certainly remind them of the potential results of youth unemployment problem and remind them of the fact that benefits of young people should also be taken into consideration in their debates on other important issues.

Fourthly, companies.

In faced with youth unemployment crisis, why would companies also need information support? This is indeed a question since they are typically considered as information providers, such as collaborating with education providers to let these institutions know which skills are expected from young people.

However, we are a community with shared interests, and in faced with youth unemployment crisis, none could be immune for it, even for companies. If companies possess more information about young people, information asymmetry will be reduced, and this will make their recruitment easier, which will benefit both companies and young people.

Fifthly, people older than 25.

People older than 25 are not included in the calculation of youth unemployment rate but they could also benefit from more information, and the information they need will be similar to that of younger people. Failing to secure a job at young age is a problem but nothing is doomed,

The information needed

and unemployed people older than 25 could also achieve their success If they choose a direction suits them and work hard enough later in their lives.

Now, what about other stakeholders? Are there any other stakeholders that should contribute to the tackling of youth unemployment problem and could benefit from the support of information?

Professor Vogel has also mentioned NGOs, NPOs and Entrepreneurs in his framework of stakeholders of youth unemployment[98]. These stakeholders may play important roles, yet their roles are less certain, and thus their influence to youth unemployment problem wouldn't be as certain as that of other stakeholders. And thus, I won't prepare information for them intentionally in the coming part of discussing information needed. Different from professor Vogel, I will use figure 8.1 to illustrate the relationship among different stakeholders—they are correlated, interacted and governments cover them all.

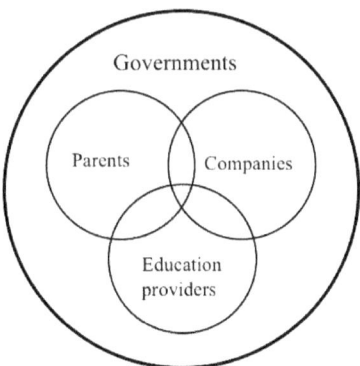

Figure 8.1 Stakeholders other than young people

8.3 Information needed for the youth (1)

During my analysis of youth unemployment problem, I've stressed the importance of preparation, which means to prepare for employment years before actually seeking employment. And I've also stressed that in order to prepare well, young people need the support of information.

Now, when it comes to discuss about what information should be provided, we must first figure out what's the implication of preparing early and the support of information? Does this mean that as long as children possessing adequate information, they could get whatever types of jobs they would like to do when they grow up?

Certainly not and it won't be so simple in reality, since there are always uncertainties and there won't be perfect information.

The poor will definitely suffer from unemployment? Nope. The rich will certainly have a prosperous future? Nope. Is it doubtless that those who fall behind at a young age can never catch up with others in the future? Nope. Then, concerning the information needed for the youth...should we just show them the fluctuations of youth unemployment rate and tell them they need to be positive, to study hard and work hard? Unfortunately, neither could we tell young people what they need to do, nor should we.

On one hand, seeing is believing. It is embedded in the nature of human being that to live in a way we believe is right rather than what other people believe is right, through which process we will form our own opinions of life. This is especially true for the youth. Young people simply won't follow the instructions of older people, and they will act in their own way—this is life. They learn from their own experience and grow by making mistakes, and this is the nature of human beings. French words '*Si les jeunes savaient, si les vieux pouvaient*' has indicated the difficulty of letting young people follow rules that the older people consider as important, and so is the sentence that '*Youth is wasted on the young.*'

On the other hand, if young people completely comply and we successfully restrict them to do what we like—rather than what they like, we may waste their talents and deprive them of their enthusiasm, which might cause harm to their future. Besides, what older people think are right may not always be right, and the change of era has made it difficult to predict how long one idea will remain useful. One case on this aspect is that the Oracle of Omaha, Warren Buffett, used to avoid investing in high-tech companies, and thus missed star companies like Google, Amazon and Alibaba. The older could help young people make their decisions, but they shouldn't decide for them.

As a result, when we talk about information needed for the youth, we should only focus on a few specific areas: to help them build their strengths and meantime convince them of avoiding mistakes that are irreparable—which may ruin their future.

To compete in job market, young people must form their own strengths, which are their competitive advantages over others. This doesn't mean that they must become top one in the world on one specific area, since there are so many companies and opportunities. What they need to do is to become excellent on one or several areas within a limited group of population, which could help employers differentiate them and hire them. From this aspect I've proposed the importance of accumulating positive signals, and there are some general signals such as education diploma. However, there are also other signals on different areas, which require many different sorts of skills and none could have them all. In fact, while there are countless signals, one can only obtain a few of them, and this means beyond some common ones, young people must form their unique signals.

This relates to direction, and the direction is more likely the interest of the youth. When young people find their interests, their passion and energy would be stimulated, which would promote them to become more determined, disciplined and responsible. When employers interview a candidate, while they will first notice signals rather than what kind of person the candidate is, young people should first identify their interests and then focus on their interests to accumulate signals. Employers first notice signals because signals are more standardized and trustworthy, but for the youth, their developing signals is closely related to their interest, and only follow their interest would those signals become easier to obtained. I state youths need signals to find a job doesn't mean they need to become a combination of tags or labels, but they must accumulate signals during their growing up, on the road of becoming better.

Everyone is unique yet at school, they learn standardized subjects and are evaluated on the same set of criteria, which do not provide them with enough opportunities to explore, identify and develop their own interests. For many children, they could find their interests and passion through other channels, but for the larger group of children, they may not have the chance to be aware of their interests for their lack of resources to help them explore more and understand more. This is the deficiency of current education system and where more information could do some good.

In this aspect, information provided could include books and researches on interest issue, opportunities for professional tests such as DISC, MBTI and Holland Codes tests, descriptions about different types of professions and may even help young people to try and experience different professions. Anyhow, we should provide information to let young people understand the importance of interests, to help them find their interests and develop their interests.

For young people that suffer from a lack of wealth and information, when they are aware of their own interests, they would find their passion and their skills will develop faster and more naturally. As they become more skilled, they will accumulate more positive signals, which will help them better prepare for their future employment. At the same time, as they have more successes, their confidence will grow, and their attention will gradually turn to learning and growing, and as long as they keep moving forward in certain areas, not only their employment prospects but also their life will become better.

Before finishing this section, there is one thing that should be highlighted. We know it is important to follow one's interest, but we do not compel young people to follow their interests and it isn't a problem if they have no idea about their sincere interests. There are so many people who know little about themselves at the time they first enter job market yet have had pretty good jobs and have remarkable achievements later in their careers. To understand and follow their interests will make it easier for them to accumulate signals, but if young people could accumulate enough signals that help them find jobs, it is well enough.

8.4 Information needed for the youth (2)

Young people learn and grow by making mistakes, but they should avoid mistakes that are irreparable, sort of mistakes that would deprive them of their opportunities and stop their personal development. And here in this section, let's focus on "mistakes".

Which kinds of mistakes are so powerful?

When we read stories of successful people, we may be confused by the fact that they come from various backgrounds, which makes it hard to find a uniform clue that could explain their successes. Some of them born in rich yet some of them born in poor, some of them were not so skilled when they were young and there are even some NBA stars used to have physical problems such as the fact that Stephen Curry once troubled by ankle problem...It seems that I have proposed a question with no answers.

If we cannot think of an answer directly, let's consider an alternative question that what factor would make an originally successful person lose his power, influence and wealth?

This is a much easier question, and we could quickly come up with a word—scandal. Scandals have the power to end politicians' political life, get CEOs kicked off by their companies and ban athletes from taking part in competitions again. For those whose scandals burst out, their life and work might be affected, since their reputation has been destroyed and no one can trust them. Now we have identified another word—reputation.

Reputation matters much for we as people in our career because it is known to all that different from laws, regulations or policies, people are various, complicated and people's behaviors are hard to predict, but how could we work with someone that is mysterious for us? Faced with such problems, good reputation provides a useful guideline that tells us while we know little about one person, he is reliable and accountable, and thus we could work with him even if we don't know them. Reputation relates to whether we are predictable for other people and are trustworthy for them, and thus matters to our successes. How could one succeed and keep making progress when nobody trusts him or is willing to support him?

Illness could be treated with medicines and the poor may get welfare and scholarship when they meet certain criteria. A lack of skills could be altered through keep practicing and macroeconomic downturn will reverse sooner or later. However, the loss of reputation could hardly get remedied. Once again, review the words by Warren Buffet that "It takes 20 years to build a reputation and 5 minutes to ruin it. If you think about that, you'll do things differently." And this is definitely what young people should bear in mind.

In the former part of this book, I've stressed the importance of having a job when young people first enter job market. While this is important, it is not so important as something that would deprive their opportunities and stops them from growing in the future. But the loss of reputation does have such power, since in our human society, our successes rely heavily on our interaction with other people and if we are not trusted, opportunities would disappear. Our society is developing faster and faster year by year, and year by year our life is becoming better and better. As long as one has good reputation, he could keep growing along with the development of society, and once their reputations collapse, their growths will very likely stop.

We learn by making mistakes, but we should avoid mistakes that would harm our reputation, and this is especially important for the youth since when they are young, they may not have such kind of sense and are not aware of the implication of their behaviors. Now we have found the answer to the question that I propose in the beginning of this section, that the loss of reputation may deprive people of their chances of success and stop them from continuously growing in their lives.

Up to now, the information that we believe young people need has focused on the aspect of themselves, including discovering their interests and avoid irreparable mistakes, which could be understood as accumulating good signals and protecting their reputation. However, to get a good job, it is not enough just possessing good signals and a good reputation, since employment involves two parties, and young people must adapt to the actual situation in job market—and this is where more information is needed.

Firstly, we need to convince them of the rules of our society, since the operation of society relies on rules and only if one acknowledges and respects rules, would they proceed with little hindrance, grow more quickly and happier. For example, companies setting up criteria for them to select their candidates, and only those who meet their criteria would get offers. And thus, in order to get offers, young people may not be able do whatever they like to do, but must figure out the requirements of companies, and respect these requirements. In another case, a hospital may establish certain procedures for patients seeking medical advice, and thus no patient should expect to see the doctor once they enter hospital but may need to make an appointment first and wait for some time.

Here I don't want readers to get misunderstood about the word "rules", and what I want to stress is more likely the sense of respecting other people, especially in things that are managed by them. From two cases proposed above, readers may find that to follow rules also means we respect other people, and the rules that I've used here mainly refer to a habit that when we deal with other people in things managed by these people, we must also pay attention to the needs and requirements of them instead of just focusing on the needs of ourselves. When young people behave in this way, they will get welcomed by other people and are more likely to succeed. In a word, this is a practice of seeking win-win result in their pursuits.

Besides the sense of respecting other people, young people are expected to possess some more concrete knowledges, such as having a basic understanding about job market, including the characteristics of various types of jobs, situations in job market such as unemployment rates, and career stories of other people. When there is adequate information on these areas, the younger generations will have a clue about the environment that they are expected to work in, and this will help them better prepare for their employment.

However, we are clear that life is full of uncertainties, and only a few people could enter the industry that fit their interests when they first enter job market. As a result, while young people need to know information on job market, they should not stick to that, and they need to prepare for unexpected changes. An instructor who spent 26 years in the US Special Forces once said[99] that an undertrained guy with a positive attitude would be more likely than a well-trained yet attitude negative guy to come out of the woods alive. Here in his expression, what the instructor stresses is positive attitude, but I want to use his idea to convince young people of the fact that there are always uncertainties in life and nothing is for sure, and they need to take care of themselves and prepare for unexpected things, even during their study at school before seeking employment.

To conclude, the information that is expected to be provided to the youth focuses more on helping them get a clue about themselves and job market, and at the same time, leaves the choices of life to the youth. Besides, young people are expected to possess positive signals and protect their reputation. Meantime, they should have a clue about situation in job market, such which sectors need more people now, which they would need in order to prepare for their employment.

Remember in chapter 4, I state that recruitment could represent the core relationship between two sides of labor force—supply and demand, so as to justify my approach of using recruitment as the starting point of analyzing youth unemployment problem. Later, I propose the Recruitment Formula, which could be extended into three issues: skill-related issue, X-factor and interest-related issue. Now, when we discuss what kind of information should be provided to the youth, we find the information needed generally matches the three issues of Recruitment Formula，and I list one comparison between them in figure 8.2.

My point is that Recruitment Formula does represent the requirements of job market, and thus is reasonable.

Recruitment Formula	Information needed for the youth
Skill-related issue	Accumulate signals
X-factor	Protect reputation
Interest-related issue	Understand oneself and things in job market

Figure 8.2 A comparison between Recruitment Formula and information needed for the youth

8.5 Information needed for other stakeholders

In section 8.2, I introduce other stakeholders who should take part in coping with youth unemployment problem, and now, let's have a look at the sorts of information that they need.

1) Parents.

When we discuss information needed for the youth, there is an imbedded assumption that they are rational enough to take that information seriously. But based on former discussions, we realize that the dimension of time also matters: children are simply too young to realize all the future implications of their choices and behaviors. And this is why when we discuss stakeholders, we must include parents.

Generally speaking, information needed for parents are largely the same as that for the youth, such as situations in job market and various types of professions, and they should be aware of the importance of accumulating signals as well as protecting personal reputation. Moreover, the information provided to parents should also take into consideration of the role of parents—to raise their children.

What is the ideal home environment for children? And how much does this ideal environment relate to wealth status? These are complicated topics and I won't cover them in this book—perhaps the ideal home environment would be those that would let children feel relaxed and make them concentrate on growing. While we cannot provide specific guidelines, we could introduce some wonderful researches and stories, and people can learn from these materials by themselves. For example, "The Grant Study" is a trustworthy research program, and the finding of "It was a history of warm intimate relationships—and the ability to foster them in maturity—that predicted flourishing in all aspects of these men's lives"[100] is also inspiring.

2) education providers

Education providers are expected to know which industries need more people in the future, so as to prepare their students for that trend. This doesn't mean they should corporate with firms in that industry to set up special programs one by one, instead this requires that they let their students notice that trend and prepare them from a skill basis. After all, many different industries share the same set of skills, and thus to help students from a skill basis is not only easier but also more valuable.

Besides, to keep an eye on the trend of robot workers, machine learning, and artificial intelligence may help education providers to better prepare their students.

3) Governments

Governments are expected to know the information on youth employment situation, and this will at least make them be aware of the interests of young people during their debates of new policies that may or may not affect the benefits of young people.

4) Companies

Companies may need the information about mobility of population and thus labor force, which would help them to better arrange their recruitment plan.

5) those older than 25

They need information about job openings, whether be apprenticeships or formal employment. And when they want to set up their own businesses, we do have information on this area that they need, such as techniques as well as law requirements concerning opening one's own store.

Here in this section, I've introduced in a very brief way the information needed for other stakeholders in youth unemployment issue, and I believe information provided should also include guidance for people to take their initiatives to gather useful information from other channels, not limited to books, websites, specific education institutions, or training organizations. Modern society has greatly facilitated the transferability of information, and a proactive person will be able to find useful information by himself.

8.6 The society's strategy

We already know that young people need additional help to assist with their development and I have discussed briefly about information needed for young people as well as other stakeholders. And now, let's have a look at what our society as a whole should do to cope with youth unemployment problem—the strategy of our society.

Youth unemployment problem comes as one crisis, but it may also serve as a great opportunity, an opportunity to conquer youth unemployment problem and alleviate wealth inequality—which requires the efforts of the whole society.

In the end of chapter 5, I conclude that youth unemployment problem is one part of wealth inequality problem, but this doesn't mean that if there is no wealth inequality, there is no youth unemployment. Recall that youth unemployment happens for lacking wealth and information, and if the amount of wealth and information available to each child remains the same yet below some certain level, these children may still suffer from unemployment, because they still lack wealth and information. Consider another situation when there exists wealth inequality—the rich are much richer than the other group of people, youth unemployment rate may still be low if the poorest of them have adequate wealth to support their development. As a result, an explicit explanation of the statement that youth unemployment problem is one part of wealth inequality is that if everyone has enough wealth, there will be no youth unemployment problem.[i]

What should the society to then? Or in other words, what would be the strategy if the society wants to do something to prevent youth unemployment crisis from recurring in the future?

From my point of view, this strategy should be divided into two parts, that one is related to wealth and the other is related to information. Figure 8.3 exhibits the relationship between three factors: level of wealth, level of information and the employment prospect of young people. Noticing that this relationship is just a rough exhibition of the general situation, which hasn't been validated by researches or proved by empirical evidences, and thus only serve as a guideline to encourage on-going researches.

In figure 8.3, the abscissa axis measures the level of wealth available to

---

[i] Remember that this book neglects the fact that there may be an excess supply of youth labor than demand of youth labor

young people during their growing process, and the ordinates axis measures the employment prospect of young people. On basic principle is that as the level of wealth rises, employment prospect of young people rises. Besides, there are three stages which are denoted as A, B and C respectively, and the slope of the line in these three stages are different, which is due to the difference among effectiveness of information altering employment prospect.

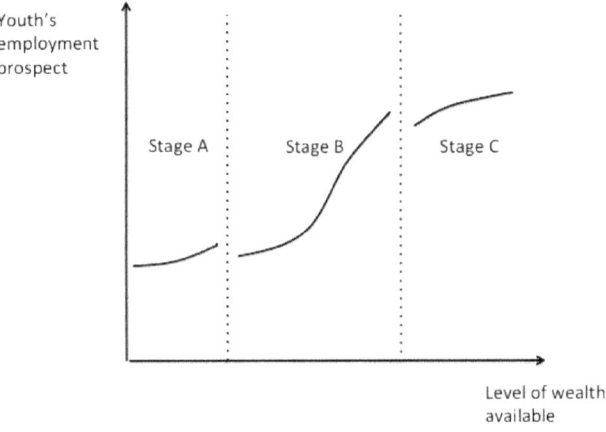

Figure 8.3 An exhibition of the likely relationship between young people's employment prospect and their level of wealth

In stage A, the slope is relatively small and somewhat stable within different wealth levels and this reflects the fact that when people's wealth is below some certain level, their first goal is to make a living, which leaves few attention or energy for the purpose of personal development. As wealth status reaches the second stage, stage B, the effectiveness of information altering employment prospect rises significantly and when it comes to stage C, this effectiveness slow down but employment prospect is still rising—which is similar to the description in physics that when acceleration falls yet remains higher than 0, the speed keeps increasing.

In stage C, the amount of wealth has reached above a certain threshold, and the effectiveness of information falls, but the employment prospect of this stage as a whole is still higher than the other two stages, reflecting the fact that as people's wealth exceeds certain high threshold, their choices of employment is significantly different than the general public: they could get access to the best education, join the board of family businesses, invest in other people's businesses or simply do not work. Compared with people in stage A and stage B, people in stage C have much more choices concerning employment.

For the purpose of easing youth unemployment and reducing wealth inequality, people in stage A and stage B should be our society's focus, and they need help relating to wealth and information. To be more specific, the society's strategy is to try best to increase the wealth of people in stage A and provide information support to people in stage B and stage A—to guarantee a minimum level of wealth for everyone plus sufficient information support for them.

To provide information support for people in stage A is also important, since based on current knowledge and practices, it is difficult to guarantee everyone the minimum wealth status, not to mention the large amount of people around the world who still live below the poverty line. Besides, even if there is a mechanism that could increase everyone's wealth to a level in stage B, this process requires time which may be very long, and while the society as a whole could wait for its completion, young people cannot wait that long. As a result, when we are trying to design an information-supporting mechanism, both people in stage A and stage B should be included as the target population.

Ideally speaking, through the interaction between information and wealth, abundant information will make people in stage A and B better prepare for employment, and thus improve their employment status as well as wealth status later in their lives. The poor will gradually become less poor, and the percentage of population in middle class will significantly expand, which will ensure the stability and development of the human society as a whole.

Readers may wonder that what are the levels of wealth that differentiate stages A, B and C? I do not provide specific data on this aspect because it requires another set of researches and may not be able to reach a conclusion within a short period of time. Besides, without these data we could still help the youth, since this book mainly proposes solutions from the perspective of information.

However, for the level of wealth that differentiates stage A and B, while I do not provide a specific figure, I do find some similar descriptions. For example, on 5th Oct 2015, the World Bank proposed a new international poverty line, which is $1.9 per day. This data may only serve as a rough measurement for our purpose here in this book and is expected to be much smaller than the threshold that differentiates A and

B, which is because the formulation of this international poverty line smooth out the differences among different countries and does not include the need for education and personal development.[101]

Besides this international poverty line, we could find many other figures. For instance, in his TED speech[102] titled *Poverty Isn't A Lack of Character; It's A Lack of Cash*, Rutger Bregman introduced that the Basic Income for the USA is $175 billion, and according to the number of people lived in poverty calculated by the US Census Bureau, 43.1 million[103], the basic income needed for each poor is around $4,060 per year, thus $11.2 per day. Is this an appropriate measure of threshold that differentiates stage A and B? Very likely but I'm not sure, and at least other countries should be very careful when they use this figure.

Noticing that my suggestion of guaranteeing a minimum level of wealth plus sufficient information support is similar to this Basic Income suggestion, except that in my suggestion there is the second part—information support. I believe this second part is at least as important as the first one and let me explain why.

To illustrate his idea of Basic Income, Rutger Bregman uses Douphin, a small town of Canada as a successful example. Would there be another successful case? And what if the practice of Basic Income is applied to the whole Canada and even the whole world?

While its uncertainty, one thing is for sure, that the practice of Basic Income wouldn't be as successful as it has been for a small town. This is because when the practice is applied to the whole world, the competition in total will rise significantly, which will definitely reduce the advantage that people in Douphin once have compared to people in other regions, and so do their employment competencies. As a result, even if everyone has some basic income, they face the same competition and their employment status wouldn't change that much, and when their employment status does not change much, they won't be able to accumulate wealth.

As more people get involved in, the logic of small sample may become more complex. This is also the problem that has appeared in McKinsey's report, which admits that "success…is scattered and small scale compared with the need"[104], with the underlying words that there is difficulty for those successful cases to cover more people. All these mean that just guarantee the basic income is not enough, and the support of information is also a needed.

Frankly speaking, the suggestion of guaranteeing basic income for

The information needed

everyone may not be achievable in the near future, but the "equality of basic information" is quite possible. In my analysis, I've focus more on the role of information and the interaction between information and wealth, which may serve as not only a more comprehensive practice but also a more practical one. This is because information does make a difference during people's growth and information is easier to share for its transferability.

9. CAREER INFORMATION CENTER

9.1 Arrangement of promoting information equality

In the former chapter, I've discussed information needed for both young people and other stakeholders, and in this chapter, let's have a look at how we should carry out our plan to promote the equality of information.

Information we are going to provide isn't secrets such as business strategies or complex knowledge such as scientific discoveries, and instead we focus on general information such as situations in job market. Specifically, we focus on "what the situation is" rather than "what should young people do" and focus on the common situation rather than individual cases. We will provide information to guide young people and their parents, but will not decide for them, since after all, young people are ultimately responsible for their future.

When information provided is more standardized rather than personalized, we should provide it by the same entity—that's the government, since to promote information equality will benefit the society as a whole and thus government has the obligation to undertake this task. And when information is provided by the government, economies of scale could be achieved, since the producing of information cost must yet the sharing of information cost little. As a practice that produces significant positive externality, it would be better for the government to implement it.

What's more, to encourage governments to provide the information needed has another implication, that people tend to trust such information. On one hand, we are actually not short of information but getting overwhelmed by useless information, and this has made it difficult to discern the information that is indeed helpful; on the other hand, as we all know that young people are used to do what they like to do, rather than what other people hope them to do. Both these two reasons have required the government to provide information, since government means "official", which also means "reliable". When it is the government that provides information, people would be more willing to trust this information.

Traditionally, governmental actions are believed to be less efficient compared with that of private sectors, but this is not true when it comes to our discussion of information equality, since to provide information requires huge investment yet the return are not certain for the information provider. We should set up a governmental agency, not only because to promote information equality and to ease youth unemployment problem is mainly a public affair, but also because this ensures that the general public could get access to credible information with little or no charge.

9.2 Implementation: career information center

To promote information equality, we should set up a public entity similar to post offices and public libraries, and I name this new public service facility as Career Information Center. Career information center aims to promote information equality among the general public.

The Career information center should be an institutional entity that has its physical workplace, with branch distributions based on population density. Similar to that of a library, career information center provides both print materials and digital materials to people who come in for information. Besides, large amount of information would be provided based on the Internet, which is efficient for not only gathering information, but also spreading information. This means the career information center is expected to have its own official website.

While web-based information may play a bigger role, manual service is an indispensable component, and often a key part. While information such as forecasted youth unemployment rate in the coming year is easy to understand, the cognitive ability of people varies, so as their ability to interpret and apply that information to their specific situation, and for some people, they will need a prepared explanation about why this piece of information matters to them. This is why just a presentation of information is not enough, and there is also a need of human support, which means there are staffs working in career information center.

Alongside with manual service we should also provide non-standardized information such as personalized career guidance if possible. Hopefully, there are career consultants working in career information center, who could use their knowledge and expertise to aid the youth in their growing process, so as to help young people better prepare for employment, or help the youth during their seeking employment, to make better choices concerning their employment. Parents used to take such roles, but many people's lack of employment have made them unable to fulfill their roles, and existing professional advisor services are often provided not for free, which makes them inaccessible for many youths. Besides, many similar services are provided exclusively to a small group of people, and for example, career services of top business schools usually serve only their students.

What's more, taking into consideration the fact that those entering job market at a young age tend to suffer more from youth unemployment problem, it would be even better if career information center could provide some basic trainings. Those who enter job market at a young age are affected adversely by the fact that they've been too young to work legally, which makes them less skilled compared with older people, and if we could help them build up some basic skills, their employment prospect would certainly improve.

Lastly, the career information center could also perform as a bridge that connects labor supply and labor demand, which means we could pose both job-demanding information and job-seeking information on its official website, or post interlinkages to relevant websites, such as LinkedIn. This would increase transparency within job market, and thus would contribute to the match of two sides of labor force: young people and companies.

This is the portrayal of the career information center, which is expected to have its physical entity as well as official website, is expected to provide both standard information and personalized guidance, and is expected to provide manual service, career advisor service and some basic skill-building services. In fact, there are currently public agencies that perform a similar role like that of career information center, just as those mentioned in MCG's report, in countries like England, Germany and India. For these countries, the setup of career information center could be based on existing facilities.

However, while their similar functions, there is one crucial deficiency of existing facilities, that they focus on the time point that young people entering job market to seek employment and won't help much for the younger population. Let's use an analogy of football game to understand this. If we consider getting a job offer equals to scoring a goal, and the role of existing career service providers is like that of the player who gives the last pass to the goal-scorer, who would get recorded by one "assist" for the score. But we know that this last pass isn't the whole story of the score, since if the ball has been intercepted and taken by players from the opponent team, there won't be this last pass, not to mention the final score. Existing career services focus too much on the last pass to the goal-scorer, with little or no attention paid to the long process before that, and this has reduced their effectiveness for the youth.

Just as stressed in this book, the past affects the future and reasons for having no jobs relate to not only the time they seek employment, but also the period long before they enter job market. To promote information equality and make everyone benefit from this information-boosting mechanism, we should not only focus on the last pass and hope to get recorded an assist but also pay attention to provide information support for those who are still too young to work, and ideally, to make people from all stages of life benefit from the setup of career information center.

9.3 Career Information Center and Education system

Education does play an important role in young people's employment, but I don't think we should emphasize too much on education, and people are still debating whether the mission of education is students' better employment or to cultivate responsible citizens. For me, I would rather say that employment isn't the goal of education, but the result of it, and a well-educated person would know that he needs a job[i]—and then, he will prepare himself well for employment.

Currently, most attention from the perspective of labor supply has focused on the role of school, aiming to help young people build skills by revising education systems. And what about the proposed career information center? Could its functions be incorporated into the education system, and become part of it? This seems to be a good idea, since schools already take a similar role and by basing functions of career information center on the infrastructure of education system, there will be a significant cost saving. However, I prefer an organizational structure independent of educational system, and let me explain why.

The first reason relates to the scale of youth unemployment problem.

We agree that youth unemployment problem is serious and requires special attention, but the description "serious" is concluded mainly by comparing current youth unemployment rate with historical youth unemployment rates. And if we have a look at youth unemployment

---

[i] Not applicable for the super-rich or those who have other sources of income

problem from the perspective of whole society, we would find that while its severity, it is less of a problem for the whole generation of young people—even at its highest level, youth unemployment rate overall is smaller than 15%, and thus smaller than 7.5% when taken into account those study at school[i], which means much more youths could find employment and many with pretty good ones.

Should we change the mechanism that works well for most youths for the reason that a much smaller group of youths cannot benefit from it? Likely not, and the suggestion of revising education system is just one kind of such trying, which should not be carried out unless obtaining support from thorough analyses and experiments. We simply cannot risk the future of most youths for the benefits of a smaller group of youths.

The second reason relates to the relationship between wealth and youth unemployment problem.

One of key conclusions of this book is that youth unemployment problem is part of wealth inequality problem. Since education requires tuition, wealth inequality will also reflect on the education that one could get access to—while there are public schools with no fee or little fees, they cannot accommodate all youths. And if there will be an addition of career information center for schools, it is almost certain that those schools with higher charges will be the first since higher charges means these school are better able to allocate additional resources, which is a must to cover expenses for the operation of career information center.

As a result, adding career information center to current education system is more likely an effort to help the rich and contribute little to the development of the poor—who are supposed to be the main target of new mechanism since they cannot afford tertiary education and suffer the most from youth unemployment problem. The setting up of career information center based on the infrastructure of educational system would contribute little to the goal of promoting information equality among the general public, because not everyone could get access to it.

The third reason relates to the difference between the role of education and that of career information center, with the latter much more employment-oriented.

---

[i] As is mentioned in chapter 2, youth unemployment ratio is typically less than half of youth unemployment rate

The experience in school[i] generally doesn't lead to a certain result, and those readings, discussions as well as activities will gradually make a person more mature, which is necessary for a responsible citizen to participate in modern life. But for career information center, the goal is clear and direct, which is to help people better prepare for employment. If we make education system emphasize too much on employment—an expected thing that within the awareness of human beings, the stability as well as advancement of human society may be harmed, since we human beings as a whole may become less capable of dealing with unexpected changes and our innovative nature may be suppressed for employment-oriented education. To turn the whole education system towards career training may bury a time bomb for our human society, which is too risky for us.

Let's understand this by using a case based on forest ecosystem. We could afforest very quickly by planting the same kind of trees, but if there is only one species in the forest, the risk that the forest being destroyed would be high, since when trees in the forest are completely identical, any problem could easily get spread to other trees. While the odds of one specific problem may be small, odds of problems may not be small since there are too many problems that could destroy a tree, such as earthquakes, wildfires, climate changes, or injurious insects. But for a forest with many different kinds of plants, there forms a complex ecosystem, and this would make the forest better capable of coping with disasters. Due to the diversity of species, the forest could handle more problems and thus is much more stable than the forest with only one species.

The role of education for individuals is similar to that of building a complex system, to make people live a good life, which is not restricted to having a good job, and this is different from the aim of career information center, which is focused on employment. School education lays the basis for employment, but they are not the same thing, since after all, life is not only about employment.

Different from education system, the role of career information center is to help young people better deal with employment issue. Young people still need to adapt to the uncertainties of life and even if they devote all their energies to one area, they may still fail, no matter how well informed or how well prepared they are. Career information center tells people what job market is and encourages them to pursue their goals but does not guarantee any result, similar to the sentence often seen in research analysts' reports that investment has risk and their

---

[i] Unless professional ones such as MBA or EMBA programs

reports do not guarantee returns. What people should expect from career information center are the things in job market, the situation of job market, and they must take initiative to pursue their goals. And for some people, simply the awareness of not taking proper employment for granted would help much.

The setup of career information center wouldn't be a dramatic change, but an adjustment based on current systems, a supplement to current public infrastructures. It should be independent of current facilities—schools, companies and welfare facilities, so as to guarantee the achieving of its objective: promoting information equality among the general public. And this means, we are not going to incorporate career information center into education system.

MCG's survey reveals that to help graduates get proper employment is not the top priority for education providers, and there is a distinction between academic education and vocational education. I consider these two things as reasonable and rational, since even if young people possess certain techniques through hands-on trainings, they could still be replaced by other people or even machines—without the ability to keep learning and growing, possessing entry-level techniques means little for competing in today's job market.

9.4 Other concerns relating to career information center

One concern relates to the density of career information centers.

Density matters because people tend to stay in career information center for a period just like they do in a library, and if there are not enough branches in one area, the goal of promoting information equality will be affected. But the density should not be too high, since while people's stay tends to be long, the frequency of their seeking information would typically be low. And they may obtain messages such as unemployment rate online, not limited to the official website of career information center. As a result, the density of career information center should neither be too high nor too low.

There are many factors that would affect the density of career information center. One factor is population, and there should be more branches for an area with larger population. Another factor is the age structure of the area. Areas where there are more young people should set up more branches than areas where there are more old people, and this is because there are much more uncertainties in young people's career prospects, which means they need more information. Besides, the level of poverty should also affect the density of career information center, with poorer areas setting up more, and this is because the information disadvantage for poor people tend to be higher, which leads to the need of more information.

The second concern relates to the effectiveness of career information center.

Traditionally, guidance and information about employment for children come from their parents, and to bring up children is a very complex and demanding task. Career information center is expected to provide information support to those who need it but would not be responsible for the growth of these children. One thing that I have stressed is that career information center shows more about "what the reality is", leaving "what to do" to young people and their parents. Even though it is expected to have career consultants working in career information center, from whom young people could seek advice, young people's actions are still up to themselves.

Would adequate information support be as effective as is expected? I am not sure, and to which level this information support could help future generations remains obscure. However, one thing is clear that the setting up of career information center would remind young people of the importance of preparing for their employment, and when they realize this at a young age, they tend to be more confident and could perform better, which is mainly because when they do not fall behind too much at a young age, they have the hope of catching up with others, and where there is hope, there is confidence, motivation and energy.

The third concern relates to entrepreneur spirit.

To encourage young people to become competent for employment should be highlighted more compared with entrepreneurship. The rationality is that to create one's own business is generally both harder and risker than being an employee, and if many youths are considered by employers as not competent for employment, how could we expect that they would succeed in creating their own businesses? Skills and competencies required of creating one's own business would be much more demanding than that of being an employee, and if competencies of the youth are not qualified for employment, we cannot suppose they are competent enough to operate their own business, not to mention that in order to launch a business, there is in need of many external factors beyond one's own competencies, such as capital investments and business connections.

Babies learn to crawl before walking and master walking before running, and this is the same for young people: the society should recognize the difficulty of young people starting their own businesses and do not take this as the top priority for tackling youth unemployment problem—even if it is important, it is not more important than seeking employment. In fact, based on administrative data sets from the U.S. Census Bureau, Azoulay et al. (2018) concluded that the average age of a successful startup founder is 45[105]. So, the group of people who should highlight entrepreneur spirit are those entrepreneurs—to encourage them to expand their businesses, so as to create more job opportunities for young people.

The fourth concern relates to the needs of current unemployed youths, which could be simplified by analyzing the relationship between possessing fish and being able to fish.

There's an ancient Chinese saying stating that teaching one to fish is better than giving him fish, which means compared with giving a person some fish, it is better to teach him how to fish, since fish will only help the hungry person for a few hours, and sooner or later, fish received will run out of storage and he will again suffer from hungry. But if he knows how to fish, he could catch some fish whenever he is hungry, in which case there would be no worry about hungry.

Similarly, efforts to help today's unemployed youths could be divided into these two categories, with helping them become more competent for employment is to teach them how to fish and to create more job positions to allocate them is to give them some fish. Up to now, this book has focused on helping future youths to become more competent for employment and discussed little about creating more job positions. This means this book has largely ignored the situation of current unemployed youths.

There is rationality for this arrangement, but this doesn't mean that we do not need to create more jobs for today's unemployed youths and in fact, we should take every chance to provide more job positions to them. Currently, to create more job positions should be prioritized, since those unemployed youths need jobs to help them build skills, which would prevent them from falling into long-term unemployment. I haven't discussed much in this area, not because it isn't important, but because I take the perspective of labor-supply to analyze youth unemployment problem from a long-term perspective.

9.5 Career information center and the arrangement for today's unemployed youths

In chapter 3, I've suggested the necessity of analyzing youth unemployment problem from the perspective of labor supply, and proposed three rationalities, with one rationality supported by one case that many young people dropped out of labor force for being unable to find employment as they entered job market during Japan's 1990 stock market crash. And we have also known the potential adverse effects caused by short-term unemployment as have been proposed by many researches. All these lead to one conclusion that today's unemployed youths need jobs right now, and this makes the practice of providing more apprenticeships and jobs an indispensable component of our mission of conquering youth unemployment problem.

For the needs of current unemployed youths, we must provide more jobs, even though this wouldn't be able to last long for its dependency on fiscal support. In the long run, the boost of job positions should not be abandoned, but should be adjusted, so as to make it a sustainable mechanism—one key issue is to reduce its dependency on funds from government.

To build a sustainable mechanism of job creation, approaches may be different but the rationality behind those approaches would be the same: jobs created based on businesses' needs, which further derive from customers' needs. Customers need products and services to fulfill their needs and only when customers pay money to buy those products and services, businesses' investment would pay off. And only when money received from customers exceeds the cost of business, would entrepreneurs' business be sustainable, so is the mechanism of job creation.

As a result, the philosophy of creating jobs continually is to target at people's needs, and one practical way for job creation is to identify what needs people have yet not been fulfilled, or what problems have bothered certain groups of people. And for the talented, to predict what needs people have yet being unaware of would be an effective way to establish and expand their businesses, just as what Apple has done for its mobile devices, iPhone and iPad for example.

To prevent youth unemployment crisis from reoccurring in the future, I have proposed the setting up of career information center, and for the operation of numerous facilities of career information center, employees are needed—job positions are created. Due to the public nature of career information center, it is likely that no fees are charged, but government shouldn't be hesitated for the cost of career information center, since these costs could be covered by the saving of welfare expenses that would be needed to support unemployed people, not to mention the increased potential economic output. The operation of career information center needs employees and today's unemployed youths need jobs, and how about we train and hire today's unemployed youths to work in career information center?

Young people's working in career information center would contribute to the fall of youth unemployment rate, and this suggestion is practical from the perspective of job requirements. This is because there is generally no threshold for most job positions in career information center[i], since the knowledge and information about job market is readily available. Besides, those unemployed young adults have an advantage over other people to fulfill their roles in career information center: they share similar experience. They know what children are thinking about at a young age, and they know the feeling of unemployment, and thus, when children come to seek help from them, they could understand the story of those children and are more likely to provide information that is needed for those children.

While its desirability, there are many potential difficulties for this arrangement. One key concern relates to whether those young people could fulfill their roles in career information center, which is especially a problem when we realize that there are many uncertainties for these tasks. On one hand, there is a lack of established knowledge about what to suggest to children, which would need to accumulate through practices. On the other hand, the effectiveness of service in career information center could hardly be observed, and there hasn't been established indicators telling us whether or not this service is trustworthy or helpful, which is complicated by the fact that the effect of information may only appear years later.

While there are worries and difficulties, this allocation of unemployed youths is still a suggestion that's worth further discussion. If, as has been argued by many researchers, that young people do not like positions below their expectations, we may not have all the candidates we want. And of course, we wouldn't hire everyone to work in career information center, and there is still a recruitment process, through which we would select the right people. Besides, if career information centers are to set up, supports from research institutions, business operations, communities and even the whole society are needed. This is a task that would benefit the whole society, and a joint effort is rightful.

---

[i] Except for career consultants

Career Information Center

10. EXTENDED DISCUSSIONS

10.1 Three guidelines for young people

Up to now, the analysis of this book has finished and when we recall the contents of my analysis, one of key ideas is to encourage young people to prepare early for employment, since the formation of skills requires time and the future depends much on the past. However, I don't want readers to overreact on this statement and the development of human beings isn't a straight line: the relationship between past and future isn't like that between chained gears and nothing could guarantee young people's future success.

We hope young people could prepare well for their employment, both mentally and technically, but this is usually not the case. What's more, while in this book the thing that I've stressed is to encourage young people to explore more about the needs of companies, I do not mean that young people should pay more attention to what job market needs than who they are. In fact, it is those who grow to become their authentic self that are more easily to find satisfying jobs, since in the process of recruitment, job seekers and recruiters are not challenging each other, but collaborating to find the find the right people for job vacancies. And thus, it is perhaps more important for job seekers to understand who they are and what they need.

Here, I'd like to propose three guidelines for young job seekers, which might help in times of confusion.

Firstly, protect your reputation.

Due to different reasons, most people would not reach their full potential during their childhood, and this is especially true for those who have been short of wealth and information. However, as children grow up, their strengths and cognitive competence will both improve. Meantime, they could travel to other places and as they get access to more people, more activities and more chances, they will have more opportunities to develop themselves, to realize their full potential gradually. But this could only happen when nothing stands against them, which means they need to protect their reputation as has been discussed before.

At the time that opportunity comes, many people just couldn't take it, not for their lack of competencies, but for their lack of reputation and no one would trust them and support them. The loss of reputation often plays a role as that of a one-veto vote, which could easily ruin all achievements that people have obtained, simply because nobody could trust them and would like to work with them. Collaboration has been highlighted in modern society and generally speaking, everyone needs support from other people, and this is why the loss of reputation could easily stop the learning and growing of people and may deprive them of their future success. While it's not clear that what would certainly damage one's reputation, and there are cultural differences in this issue, to abide by law would certainly contribute to the protection of reputation.

Secondly, to possess some basic skills and do not fall behind too much concerning the right set of skills.

Besides reputation, young people are also expected to possess certain skills, which is the basis for their contribution to the operation of companies.

In reality, employers do welcome highly skilled graduates, which would reduce training costs and risks. This is because companies do not operate in an easy market, and a team consisting of highly skilled entry-level employees would become a competitive advantage for those companies' survival. Besides, when there are more applicants than positions, companies are able to select some from their talent pool, which would usually make it harder to get a job.

However, in most cases young people are not expected to possess a specific set of skills, or too skilled, since it is known to all that job-specific skills could only get developed from on-site experience and for a fresh graduate, a high standard requirement would be unrealistic. We could form a general insight on this issue from the global survey of McKinsey, in which data reveals that employers do have skill requirements, but those requirements are mainly general ones such as work ethic, teamwork and language skills.

Job market does not require young people to be too skilled but the nature of development of skills requires young people to be skilled to a certain degree, otherwise they may easily get depressed and then give up. On one hand, the development of skills is usually not an overnight process, but requires hard work for long periods of time, and when young people realize their lack of certain skills, they may find it hard to catch up with others. On the other hand, increased competition brings more pressure, and while people could develop their skills later at work, to learn some early would be a competitive advantage for them. Concerning the set of skills that young people should focus on, a proper answer would be that to follow their interests and meantime, to keep an eye on the trends in society, such as today's needs for data analyst skills.

Thirdly, to build a positive thinking habit and to have a strong mind.

Thinking habit matters much and at least young people should be aware of the fact that employment is a process of exchange, which means job seekers exchange their contributions for salaries and employers exchange their money for human capital. As a result, a win-win approach should be highlighted. For this part I would like to finish quickly by restating the idea made by Gordon Smith that an undertrained guy with a positive attitude would be more likely than a well-trained yet attitude negative guy to come out of the woods alive.

This is the three guidelines for young people, which could be summarized as follows: to protect their reputations, do not fall behind too much so that they won't get depressed, and to build a positive thinking habit and to have a strong mind.

10.2 Strategies for young people

When we examine the situation of young people, we find that their positions are quite similar to that of companies in the business world, that have to make progress continually and fight for their own successes. This inspires us that young people should have their own strategies of development, just as companies.

For the purpose of people's self-management, we could borrow concepts and theories from business management areas, and when we do things like this, we find that business management strategies could also be used to guide people's personal developments. In this section and next section, I will introduce two strategies that generally apply to all, which have helped many people to handle successfully situations like lacking desired job opportunities or lacking wealth during their processes of growing up. These strategies may not be perfect but will enlighten and support us and are helpful for young people.

Extended discussions

One of the basic principles of business management is to examine issues from a long-term point of view, which means to recognize the causality of activities and pay attention to the future implication of behaviors now. We could incorporate this idea in our personal strategy. For example, if one person expects in the future that his work will require a good health status, instead of giving up sports, he may join a sports team to keep fit. This sort of long-term perspective enables us to better handle short-term adverse conditions so as to achieve a balance between current needs and the needs of future.

The Boston Consulting Group (BCG), one of the world's leading strategic consulting companies, proposes a strategy framework for companies to make their strategy decisions—Strategy Palette[106]. This Strategy Palette contains five kinds of business environment that companies would face and their corresponding strategies. One of the five strategies is named as Renewal, which means companies should first focus on survival and saving resources, such as cutting off expenses, during times when their operations are in serious trouble, whether due to harsh external environment changes or due to their own problems. Only so, would they prepare well for the stage of revival.

This strategy of Renewal has important implication for today's young people, who are experiencing an economy downturn caused by financial crisis and are entering job market with fewer "good jobs". If a person enters job market at a time when only some basic jobs are available, they should take those that they are able to take up, so as to support themselves during these difficult times. They could keep learning and growing during leisure time of their work and once environment improves or they become more competent, they could apply for their desired ones. Or they may perform excellent in those basic job positions and get promoted to more important ones.

The key issue is that young people should understand that there may be unexpected changes and they may not obtain what they want, whether due to their personal incompetence of taking up their desired jobs or due to adverse environment changes that have greatly reduced the supply of such job positions. A person could experience difficult times just as a company does, during which periods self-preservation will become the top priority—they need first survive during hard periods, which would leave a chance for a better future. If, on the other hand, they refuse to take basic jobs, they will have to live on their parents or the support of social welfare and may miss the opportunity to do something to improve themselves. If so, the existence of long blank periods in their careers may reduce their chances of applying for their desired jobs in the future, when the economy improves. This is the case when economic situation is not good, and in another case, when we are not competent enough for our desired jobs, we could learn from the story of Paul Smith, whose philosophy is similar to that of BCG's renewal strategy.

Paul Smith is a leading designer in England's fashion industry, but the legend of his success started from a small clothing store. His philosophy during that period is described by himself as *Eclecticism*[107], which partly means from Monday to Thursday, he operated the small store to cover his expenses, and on Friday and Saturday, he made progress for his dream jobs, such as attending evening classes and learning designing. Six years after his opening of that store at the age of 24, he held his first fashion show in Paris. And now, we know Paul Smith is very successful and famous, which isn't affected by his situation at a young age.

The eclecticism philosophy of Mr. Smith is first to survive when not able to obtain desired jobs, whether this inability happens as a result of personal incompetence or due to external adverse environment. First survive by accepting suboptimal jobs and develop skills in case of lack of competence or wait for opportunities in case of adverse environment, and the final result would be much better than long-term unemployment and complaining about bad luck.

Where there is life, there is hope. BCG's *Renewal* strategy and Paul Smith's *Eclecticism* philosophy indicate the same thing: during harsh times, focusing on survival and keeping making progress, so as to prepare for future opportunities. And once opportunities appear, seize them and begin to revive. When there are no desired jobs, or they are not competent enough for their desired jobs, young people should take up jobs they could get access to and prepare carefully for future opportunities, and this is one strategy of personal management.

10.3 Keep investing in yourself and keep learning

We know that the poor suffer more from youth unemployment problem, but this is not for sure, and the poor still have opportunities to become successful later in their lives. However, for them to become successful, they need a special strategy, similar to the one we've introduced in the former section.

In fact, growing up in poor background could be considered as one harsh situation as we have mentioned along with BCG's *Renewal* strategy and Paul Smith's *Eclecticism* philosophy, with one difference being that living in poor is a much longer period of difficulty, and thus would require greater efforts in order to succeed later. During difficult times, people may not be able to enjoy leisure time as often as other people do but must work hard and keep investing in themselves, in which way to become more and more competent, to earn themselves a better future. People in hard times are expected to be more focused and keep investing in their personal development.

Here are lessons from NBA. Many super stars grow up in poor backgrounds, but they succeed later, earn hundreds of millions of dollars and become famous all over the world. When we read life stories of these people, we would find that they were dedicated to basketball when they were young—they kept investing the time they had to become better and stronger, which left little time for them to play games as other children did. This is the strategy—to be focused and keep investing in themselves, and become more and more competent, which finally brings great fame and huge wealth as they grow up.

What's more, when we go through those NBA stars' experience as well as their feelings very carefully, we could usually find that while they might feel embarrassed and pressured for being poor, they were happy when they played basketball and really enjoyed themselves. This means the process of giving up leisure time and keeping investing in themselves may not be as burdensome as people generally think. And the secret, relates to interest and the probability of success. For those NBA stars, they are definitely interested in playing basketball, and during their childhoods, they were much better than their peers, which means they knew when they were children that they would succeed if they kept playing hard enough.

Sports has taught us many things, but we cannot simply apply those lessons to other people directly, since sport is one special type of profession that has its own features. One feature is that whether one child is interested in sports and be able to participate in sports competition could be seen easily during their childhoods with less effort, for a reason that sports are extremely demanding for physical status.

But this is usually not the case for other professions, such as lawyers, bankers, musicians or engineers. We cannot tell what kinds of professions a child will take when he grows up, since differences between these professions are less observable compared with differences between sports and these professions. As a result, the general public need assistance to help them understand themselves better, including but not limited to their interests, strengthens and weaknesses. Ideally speaking, when a child realizes his interest, he could easily get focused and keep making progress in that area, and when this interest relates to one type of profession, he could get succeed quicker than the general public, just as those NBA stars do.

In her book *Nickel and Dimed: On (Not) Getting by In America*, Barbara Ehrenreich exhibits how hard life is for the unskilled working poor: ordinary jobs with no hope for success. While it is, there's still a chance if these people who are doing ordinary jobs have their own development strategies, just like Paul Smith did in his twenties. Or they may be able to avoid such ordinary jobs if they began to prepare for their careers at a much younger age, early enough for them to develop the right set of skills. Even if those currently working poor may not become wealthy in their later stages of life, they still have incomes and if their children get enough support and perform better than them, their situation will also improve in the future.

The key for the poor to become successful is to be more focused than the general public and spend a larger portion of time as well as wealth in their personal developments. In the former section I suggest that those who have been suffering from a lack of wealth could still succeed later in their careers, and in most cases that I've read, those people have done an excellent job during their studies and obtained degrees from top universities. They wouldn't achieve this if they were not focused and this is the right strategy for those who are not satisfied with their situation: to be focused and keep investing in themselves, so as to make them deserve what they want. If they have no ideas about their interests and do not know which areas to focus on, to study hard and do as good as they could at school might be the right choice, since for young people who have little work experience, excellent academic achievements would be the best signals that could remind employers of how competent these candidates are.

10.4 A new angle of understanding wealth inequality

Wealth inequality has always been a key issue in our human society.

Right now, the understanding of wealth inequality has generally taken a macro perspective and relies heavily on statistical charts, such as plotting wealth data against timeline to show its movements through the years. This method helps since it helps people form a basic understanding about the situation of wealth inequality quickly. One example is Piketty's bestseller *Capital in the 21th Century*, which contains many charts and one chart shows trends of share of wealth possessed by the richest 1%

population.

However, queries never end for that book and one issue is the validity of data. One example is the debate between Thomas Piketty and the Financial Times, especially economics editor of FT, Chris Giles. Here I am not going to conclude who wins the debate, but I would like to point out a generally acknowledged idea that data may be misleading. For example, the mean value of a set of numbers—1, 2, 3, 4, 5, 6, 210—is 33, and if we conclude based on this mean value that each number in the array is near 33, we are wrong. We are wrong because the calculation of mean value is easily affected by extreme values, such as 210 in this case. Median may be a better indicator of the actual situation in this array, and the median is 4, through which we know numbers in the array generally distribute around 4.

We could not reach out to the actual situation if we just look at summarized data, in which case we may get misled by what we see. There is one principle for economic analysis that we need to find the theoretical basis for our empirical research, otherwise the result of empirical study may just appear occasionally and could not be considered as a proof of causal relationship between different variables.

In an article published on the website of the Fortune, Erik Sherman(2015) relates data from Allianz and states that while wealth inequality problem is severe in the USA, there exists economic mobility, and "70% of the population experiencing at least 1 year in the top 20% of income and 53% landing in the top 10% in at least 1 year."[108] When we take this mobility into consideration of the likely fact that while the richest have become richer, many people become part of the richest one year and then drop out. If so, we find wealth inequality doesn't constitute a huge problem since everyone is equal, and the only difference is in which year they will become one part of the richest.

Of course, the actual situation won't be such simple and not everyone has the opportunity to experience what it feels like to be extremely rich. Here through this case, the thing I want to stress is the necessity of analyzing wealth inequality issue from a micro perspective, which gets down to individuals and the actual process that people make their fortune and accumulate wealth.

The new angle of understanding wealth inequality is to take the perspective of people—after all, it is people that possess capital, labor or management talent, and they utilize these resources to make a fortune. When we take the angle of individuals to understand wealth inequality, we could focus on the actual process that people accumulate wealth, such as investment activities. And when we get down to the actual processes, we would find that people can also lose money in their investments. In *Capital in the 21th Century*, Piketty states that wealth inequality results from the difference of returns between capital and labor, but when we observe the process of individuals making their fortune, we would find it's neither that easy to accumulate wealth through capital investment, nor that difficult to accumulate wealth through working for others.

For example, based on an 8-year study of corporate sustainability, researchers from MIT Sloan Management Review and the Boston Consulting Group state that "Most types of businesses in most industries run the risk of dying younger."[109] When companies go to bankruptcy, assets of business owners will shrink, which indicates the risk and difficulty of accumulating wealth through capital investment.

Meantime, Harvard Business Review has published an article titled *Corporations in the Age of Inequality*[110], written by Nicholas Bloom, which indicates the significance of analyzing income difference within and between firms. The intent of that article is to introduce the role of companies in the formation of wealth inequality between individuals, but we could draw another conclusion that there are some people who could become super rich through employment, since not all those employees hired by high-paying companies like Google and Twitter come from rich families. This means children growing up in poverty may also become rich through working for others, and the accumulation of wealth through labor isn't always impossible.

There is a famous series of documentary films called the Up Series, which records the lives of 14 British children every 7 years, and "The children were selected to represent the range of socio-economic backgrounds in Britain at that time, with the explicit assumption that each child's social class predetermines their future."[111] However, just as one of the three children from "upper class", says in *56 Up* that the financial condition of his family has worsened since he was quite young and his mother had to work very hard to pay his private school tuition. And in fact, he finished his study at Oxford with the help of scholarship. This respected person was born rich and is still rich at his 50s, however, we could not tell it is capital that determines this result and in fact, it is hard work and the determination of living a good life that have supported him and his family.

In fact, the actual process of accumulating wealth and staying rich is much more complex than what's described by the difference between returns of capital and labor, and many events could change the economic condition of individuals or even conditions of the total population in a country. For example, in his prepared essay[112] for the annual meeting of the American Economic Association, professor Mankiw suggests that when consider the effect of consumption, procreation and taxation, wealth inherited by descendants of the wealthy is actually much smaller than what has been expected.

In people's daily lives, it is neither that easy to accumulate wealth through capital nor that difficult to make fortune through employment, and in order to have a better understanding about wealth inequality problem, we need to focus on those actual processes too.

Not only data, but also actual processes, and this is the method that I've used in this book of analyzing youth unemployment problem. To try to understand causes of youth unemployment problem from the perspective of labor supply, I focus on recruitment and propose the Recruitment Formula, with its extended version, and conclude that young people should also be responsible for their unemployment. And then, I discuss the relationship between youth unemployment problem and wealth inequality problem: youth unemployment problem exists partly for wealth inequality problem and if we could help young people get better jobs, we would help them accumulate wealth, which would provide a chance of mitigating wealth inequality in our human society.

10.5 The opportunity behind youth unemployment crisis

In his book *Capital in the 21th Century*, Piketty states that wealth inequality results from and gets reinforced by the difference between return on private capital, r, and growth rate of economy, g. Since r is much larger than g, the accumulation of wealth through capital is faster than the accumulation of wealth through labor, and as time passes, the advantage of holding capital in the beginning gets strengthened, so does the problem of wealth inequality. As a result, a progressive income taxation with the maximum marginal tax rate for those with annual income over $0.5million or $1million to be 80% and a progressive global taxation on capital are proposed.

Should these solutions be implemented? Likely not, at least not now, and even the author himself has admitted in his book that no mathematical formula except for a collective review and social experiment could indicate us which marginal rate should be set for which level of income, and it is unlikely that this sort of policies would be carried out quickly. Besides, the logic of these solutions has been questioned, since it has mixed up two critical concepts: absolute poverty and the relative inequality of wealth.

Absolute poverty and the relative inequality of wealth, which one should be prioritized in our tackling of wealth inequality problem?

Absolute poverty, I believe, should be prioritized. We should focus more on increasing income of the poor, rather than reducing income of the rich, which means we should emphasize more on ending absolute poverty rather than putting forth effort towards narrowing the wealth gap between the rich and the poor. It isn't necessary to be billionaires in order to live a good life, and what we hope is that the living standards of everyone could remain above certain level, in which case the inequality of wealth would be less of a concern when everybody lives well. In fact, life is full of uncertainties, and no one could be certain enough that nothing would happen to their fortunes. As a result, I don't think we should change current system just for the purpose of reducing income of the super-rich or narrowing the gap between the rich and the poor.

Several years after 2008 financial crisis, youth unemployment crisis becomes a global issue that attracts public attention. Many country-level mechanisms have been carried out in order to help those unemployed youths and there also emerge numerous studies and researches. Moreover, public's nerve has been stimulated and as a result, they are more willing to listen and receive messages about how to help young people. All these will help us better deal with youth unemployment problem. Besides, we already know that poverty has fostered young people's unemployment and actually, the poor suffer more from youth unemployment problem than the rich—which means, if we could take this opportunity to help the unemployed youths, we would contribute to the tackling of poverty.

Here in this book, the analysis of youth unemployment crisis has taken the perspective of labor supply, through which I state that youth unemployment problem reflects wealth inequality problem, absolute poverty problem to be specific. And there is interaction between youth unemployment and poverty: poverty leads to unemployment and unemployment reinforces poverty. As a result, if we could help young people to have better employment, their economic conditions will improve, so will the overall situation of poverty. This means, the tackling of youth unemployment will contribute to the ease of wealth inequality.

This is the opportunity behind this youth unemployment crisis: to ease absolute poverty problem, and wealth inequality problem. The poor suffer more from youth unemployment problem and during our tackling of youth unemployment, the poor benefit more, and thus the tacking of youth unemployment problem is actually in consistent with the reduction of poverty. While there may be working poverty, to have a job is at least better than no jobs. And through the bond of family as well as spirit of sacrifice between family members, the lives of future generations would become better, an effect that would get enhanced with external support such as promoting information equality. As a result, absolute poverty and wealth inequality would be eased from a long-term point of view.

THE CONCLUSION

An analysis of youth unemployment problem from the perspective of labor supply

Traditionally, policies aim at creating more job positions in times of rising unemployment rate, based on the logic mentioned in the beginning of this book that "unemployment rate measures the economy's ability to generate employment and reflects its ability to absorb labor force." However, when this practice is applied to the tackling of youth unemployment problem, it has an embedded assumption that young people are competent enough for employment and existing job opportunities have been taken up. But in reality, this assumption does not always hold, and this is why both young people and companies or even policy makers are not satisfied with some forms of job creation efforts.

To understand the occurring of youth unemployment crisis, this book has focused on young people themselves: beyond macroeconomic factors, should the youth also be responsible for their unemployment? This involves an analysis about the competencies of young people, which would constitute an essential supplement to our current knowledge about youth unemployment since economic conditions are cyclical and always fluctuate, with high uncertainty that we cannot count on—our human society as a whole may be able to cope with occasional crises led by economic fluctuations, but for individuals, their future may be destroyed just for one time of crisis.

The method I use is to target at recruitment and propose the Recruitment Formula, through which I reach the conclusion that many youths are not competent enough for employment. In other words, young people haven't prepared well for employment, both mentally and technically. They're not ready for their lack of wealth and information during their growing up, and since for children, wealth and information come largely from family members, young people's unemployment actually reflects their family's short of wealth and information, and thus the poor suffer more from youth unemployment problem than the rich. This means that from the perspective of labor supply, youth unemployment problem exists as part of wealth inequality problem.

The solution that I propose is to guarantee everyone a minimum level of wealth with sufficient information support—to achieve information equality. In order to promote information equality among the general public, I propose the setup of career information center, a public facticity that is operated by the government. Information provided in career information center mainly relates to what facts are, including but not limited to the situations in job market, different types of jobs and what are the interests as well as strengths and weaknesses of individuals. Through sufficient information support at a young age, young people could better prepare for their future employment.

Will information equality help? I would say yes since at a young age, it is easier to develop skills, which would later be perceived as positive signals by employers, and hopefully this would help them avoid certain kinds of mistakes that may stop them from keeping learning and growing, which means young people are expected to have the awareness of protecting their reputation.

Noticing that I encourage promoting information equality doesn't mean to guarantee everyone the same level of information, but similar to the description of minimal level of wealth, and to make sure that each youth has the information he needs to know. In other words, this is an absolute value rather than a relative one. And I must clarify that types of information I have proposed in chapter 8 mainly serve as a supplement to our current knowledge and doesn't cover all that young people need to know. Young people could learn from their parents, friends, educations and experiences gradually.

Moreover, in our practice of promoting information equality, we cannot rely entirely on the setup of career information center, but should also encourage the sharing of information, such as to encourage research institutions to release more information on employment prospects and to encourage companies introduce more about their recruitment arrangements. To tackle youth unemployment, cooperation and collaboration will be needed.

And, a labor-supply side analysis of youth unemployment has naturally taken a long-term view, which targets at preventing youth unemployment crisis from recurring in the future, and this means I have generally neglected the arrangements to help today's unemployed youths. But I do suggest offering job positions in career information center, which could act as a sustainable job creation mechanism in the long run.

To get a good job is never easy, but we could borrow concepts and strategies from business management areas to help make our own strategies, since we as people have the same concern as companies: to survive and succeed in an ever-changing and competitive environment. For example, the Eclecticism philosophy of Paul Smith is quite similar to the Renewal strategy in BCG's Strategy Palette.

To conclude, youth unemployment problem is an important issue that matters to all, and to help young people requires a joint effort of the whole society. Let's unite and work together to make a prosperous future for the youth.

The conclusion

AFTERWORD

Finally, I finish this book.

I noticed youth unemployment crisis in 2013, and since then I've spent 6 years in writing this book. I hope this book could perform as a supplement to current knowledge and help build a comprehensive as well as consistent framework of youth unemployment analysis.

English is not my mother language and unemployment issue is not the subject during my school study, and these have made it more difficult for me to write this book. However, I've determined to finish it since I believe that my ideas are worthwhile to share with others.

Readers who would like to provide feedback concerning contents or any other aspects of my book please contact me at: hxlland@gmail.com.

Thanks.

Xiaolong Hou

2020/01/02

ABOUT THE AUTHOR

Xiaolong Hou, is an experienced risk manager in banking industry, who has a master's degree in finance from Tongji University and a Master in Management degree from ESCP-Europe.

He loves reading and writing, and was once described as "a critical thinker, an in-depth analyst and a good writer" by a senior private banker.

BIBLIOGRAPHY

[1] Schmillen, A., & Umkehrer, M. (2018). The scars of youth: Effects of early-career unemployment on future unemployment experience. International Labor Review.Vol.156 Issue 3-4, 465-494. Available from:
https://onlinelibrary.wiley.com/doi/abs/10.1111/ilr.12079 [Accessed: 10 Oct 2019]

[2] European Commission - Fact Sheet (2015). Youth Guarantee: Questions and Answers [online]. Brussels. Available from:
http://europa.eu/rapid/press-release_MEMO-15-4102_en.htm [Accessed: 20 Aug 2017]

[3] EMCC (2013). Youth Guarantee: EU leaders intensify efforts to tackle youth unemployment [online]. Eurofound. Available from:
https://www.eurofound.europa.eu/news/news-articles/youth-guarantee-eu-leaders-intensify-efforts-to-tackle-youth-unemployment [Accessed: 20 Aug 2017]

[4] The World Bank: Unemployment, youth total (modeled ILO estimate): ILO, ILOSTAT database. Available from:
http://data.worldbank.org/indicator/SL.UEM.1524.ZS [Accessed: 21 Aug 2017]

[5] The same source as reference 4

[6] Available from:
http://www.ilo.org/ilostat-files/Documents/description_UR_EN.pdf [Accessed: 21 Aug 2017]

[7] McKinsey Center for Government, Education to Employment: Designing a system that works, December 2012. Available from:
https://www.mckinsey.com/industries/social-sector/our-insights/education-to-employment-designing-a-system-that-works

[8] The same source as reference 7, Exhibit 20

[9] The same source as reference 7, Exhibit 2

[10] The World Bank: Labor force participation rate for ages 15-24, total (%) (modeled ILO estimate): ILO, ILOSTAT database. Available from:
https://data.worldbank.org/indicator/SL.TLF.ACTI.1524.ZS [Accessed: 21 Aug 2017]

[11] Cooper, R.V.L. (1978). Youth Labor Markets and the Military [Online]. RAND Corporation. Available from: https://www.rand.org/pubs/papers/P5927.html [Accessed: 21 Aug 2017]

[12] Light, J., Weber, L. (Nov 2011). Generation Jobless: For Those Under 24, a Portrait in Crisis [online]. The Wall Street Journal. Available from:
https://www.wsj.com/articles/SB10001424052970203733504577022110945459408 [Accessed: 27 Aug 2017]

[13] Blackden, R. (Nov 2012). Youth unemployment: the big issue for the world's economy [online]. The Telegraph. Available from: http://www.telegraph.co.uk/finance/jobs/youth-unemployment-competition/9653113/Youth-unemployment-the-big-issue-for-the-worlds-economy.html [Accessed: 21 Aug 2017]

[14] OECD (2017), Youth unemployment rate (indicator). doi: 10.1787/c3634df7-en (Accessed on 21 Aug 2017)

[15] The same source as reference 4

[16] The same source as reference 14

[17] Malik, S. (Oct. 2012). Europe's lost generation costs €153bn a year, study finds [online]. The Guardian. Available from: https://www.theguardian.com/society/2012/oct/22/europe-lost-generation-costs-study [Accessed: 21 Aug 2017]

[18] Mroz, T.A., & Savage, T.H. (2001). The Long-Term Effects of Youth Unemployment [online]. Available from: https://www.epionline.org/studies/r51/

[19] Santacrose, R. (2013). Long Term Consequences of Youth Unemployment [online]. Available from: https://www.uschamberfoundation.org/blog/post/long-term-consequences-youth-unemployment/34032

[20] Kelly, E., McGuinness, S., & O'Connell, P.J., [2011]. Transitions to Long-Term Unemployment Risk Among Young People: Evidence from Ireland [online], Papers WP394, Economic and Social Research Institute (ESRI). Available from: https://ideas.repec.org/p/esr/wpaper/wp394.html

[21] The same source as reference 7, Page 11

[22] McQuaid, R. (2015) Multiple scarring effects of youth unemployment, Skills in Focus report for Skills Development Scotland. DOI: 10.13140/RG.2.1.1300.4964. Available from: https://www.researchgate.net/publication/278303095_Multiple_scarring_effects_of_youth_unemployment

[23] The same source as reference 13

[24] European Commission. Youth Guarantee[online]. Available from: http://ec.europa.eu/social/main.jsp?catId=1079 [Accessed: 21 Aug 2017]

[25] European Commission - Fact Sheet (2015). Youth Guarantee: Questions and Answers [online]. Brussels. Available from: http://europa.eu/rapid/press-release_MEMO-15-4102_en.htm [Accessed: 21 Aug 2017]

[26] G20 Leaders Statement: The Pittsburgh Summit (Sep 2009) [online]. Pittsburgh. Available from: http://www.g20.utoronto.ca/2009/2009communique0925.html [Accessed: 21 Aug 2017]

[27] Available from:

http://www.ilo.org/global/about-the-ilo/newsroom/news/WCMS_126202/lang--de/index.htm [Accessed: 21 Aug 2017]

[28] Axelrad, H., Malul, M., & Luski,I. (2018). Unemployment among younger and older individuals: does conventional data about unemployment tell us the whole story?. Journal for Labor Market Research. 2018, 52(1): 3. Available from: https://labourmarketresearch.springeropen.com/articles/10.1186/s12651-018-0237-9

[29] The same source as reference 14

[30] Peacock, L. (Jan 2012). Almost one in four apprentices drop out [online]. The Telegraph. Available from:
http://www.telegraph.co.uk/finance/jobs/hr-news/9052479/Almost-one-in-four-apprentices-drop-out.html [Accessed: 22 Aug 2017]

[31] The same source as reference 30

[32] Peacock, L. (Feb 2012). Employers warn on 'quickie apprenticeships' [online]. The Telegraph. Available from:
http://www.telegraph.co.uk/finance/jobs/9062660/Employers-warn-on-quickie-apprenticeships.html [Accessed: 22 Aug 2017]

[33] The same source as reference 30

[34] Peacock, L. (Feb 2012). One in five apprenticeships lasts for just six months [online]. The Telegraph. Available from:
http://www.telegraph.co.uk/finance/jobs/9052402/One-in-five-apprenticeships-lasts-for-just-six-months.html [Accessed: 22 Aug 2017]

[35] OWEN, V. (Jun 2014). Small firms warn funding cuts may stop the boom in apprentice jobs in its tracks and hit young workers[online]. This is MONEY. Available from:
http://www.thisismoney.co.uk/money/smallbusiness/article-2651548/Small-firms-warn-funding-cuts-destroy-boom-apprentice-jobs.html [Accessed: 22 Aug 2017]

[36] Johnson, S. (May 2012). Arnold Clark: More than 80 per cent of apprentice applicants 'unemployable'[online]. The Telegraph. Available from:
http://www.telegraph.co.uk/news/politics/9280740/Arnold-Clark-More-than-80-per-cent-of-apprentice-applicants-unemployable.html [Accessed: 22 Aug 2017]

[37] The World Bank: GDP growth (annual %): World Bank national accounts data, and OECD National Accounts data files. Available from:
https://data.worldbank.org/indicator/NY.GDP.MKTP.KD.ZG [Accessed: 21 Aug 2017]

[38] For youth unemployment rate: the same source as reference 4

[39] The same source as reference 14

[40] The same source as reference 14

[41] Youth Unemployment. Eurostat Statistics Explained. Available from:
http://ec.europa.eu/eurostat/statistics-explained/index.php/Youth_unemployment

[Accessed: 22 Aug 2017]

[42] OECD (2016), Unemployment rates by education level (indicator). doi: 10.1787/6183d527-en (Accessed: 31 Oct 2016)

[43] Youth Unemployment Rate, Figures by State. Governing. Available from: http://www.governing.com/gov-data/economy-finance/youth-employment-unemployment-rate-data-by-state.html [Accessed: 22 Aug 2017]

[44] Burrus, J., & Roberts, R. D. (2012). Dropping out of high school: Prevalence, risk factors, and remediation strategies. R & D Connections, 18, 1-9. Their explanation of factors associated with dropping out of high school has contained findings by Allensworth, 2005; Roderick, 1994 and Rumberger, 2004

[45] Tyler, J. H., & Lofstrom, M. (2009). Finishing high school: Alternative pathways and dropout recovery. The future of children, 19(1), 77-103

[46] European Commission. (Jan 2011). Early school leaving in Europe – Questions and answers (online). Brussels. Available from: http://europa.eu/rapid/press-release_MEMO-11-52_en.htm [Accessed: 22 Aug 2017]

[47] Malik, S. (Oct 2012). Europe's lost generation costs €153bn a year, study finds (online). The guardian. Available from: https://www.theguardian.com/society/2012/oct/22/europe-lost-generation-costs-study [Accessed: 22 Aug 2017]

[48] The same source as reference 36

[49] Data and descriptions of this paragraph are based on the appendices of McKinsey Center for Government, Education to Employment: Designing a system that works, December 2012

[50] McKinsey Center for Government, Education to Employment: Getting Europe's Youth into Work, January 2014. Available from: https://www.mckinsey.com/industries/social-sector/our-insights/converting-education-to-employment-in-europe

[51] The same source as reference 7, Exhibit 20

[52] The same source as reference 7, calculated based on Exhibit 13

[53] The same source as reference 7, Exhibit 2

[54] The same source as reference 7, based on info from Exhibit 12 and 13

[55] Vogel, P. (2015). Generation Jobless? Turning the youth unemployment crisis into opportunity. Palgrave Macmillan

[56] The same source as reference 47

[57] Harding, R. (Aug 2015). New World of Work: Japan's lost generation struggles to catch up [online]. The Financial Times. Available from: https://www.ft.com/content/6f1a7626-0ade-11e5-9df4-00144feabdc0 [Accessed: 22 Aug 2017]

[58] The same source as reference 7, Page 19

[59] Desai, S. (Jan 2016). What to Do When You Realize You Made a Bad Hire [online]. Fortune. Available from:

http://fortune.com/2016/01/16/made-bad-hire/ [Accessed: 23 Aug 2017]

[60] Porath, C. (Feb 2016). How to Avoid Hiring a Toxic Employee [online]. Harvard Business Review. Available from: https://hbr.org/2016/02/how-to-avoid-hiring-a-toxic-employee [Accessed: 23 Aug 2017]

[61] Housman, M., & Minor, D. (2015). Toxic Workers. Harvard Business School Strategy Unit Working Paper No. 16-057. Available from SSRN: https://ssrn.com/abstract=2677700 or http://dx.doi.org/10.2139/ssrn.2677700 [Accessed: 11 Sep 2017]

[62] Torres, N. (Dec 2015). It's Better to Avoid a Toxic Employee than Hire a Superstar [online], Harvard Business Review. Available from: https://hbr.org/2015/12/its-better-to-avoid-a-toxic-employee-than-hire-a-super star [Accessed: 11 Sep 2017]

[63] The same source as reference 62

[64] Socialization. 2017. In Merriam-Webster.com. Available from: https://www.merriam-webster.com/medical/socialization [Accessed: 11 Sep 2017]

[65] Chamorro-Premuzic, T. (2017). Could Your Personality Derail Your Career? [online]. Harvard Business Review. Available from: https://hbr.org/2017/09/could-your-personality-derail-your-career [Accessed: 24 Sep 2017]

[66] The same source as reference 50, Appendices

[67] The same source as reference 7, Exhibit 11

[68] The same source as reference 50, Exhibit 2

[69] The same source as reference 7, Exhibit 13

[70] The same source as reference 7, Exhibit 15

[71] The same as reference 71

[72] The same source as reference 7, Exhibit 6

[73] The same source as reference 7, Exhibit 4

[74] The same source as reference 50, Exhibit 15

[75] The same as reference 73

[76] The same source as reference 7, Exhibit 3

[77] The same source as reference 50, Exhibit 13

[78] The same source as reference 50, Exhibit 18

[79] Piketty, T. (2014). Capital in the Twenty-First Century. Simplified Chinese translation. Beijing: China CITIC Press

[80] Bloom, N. (2017). Corporations in the age of inequality [online]. Harvard Business Review. Available from: https://hbr.org/cover-story/2017/03/corporations-in-the-age-of-inequality [Accessed: 15 Nov 2017]

[81] For data relating to wealth inequality: OECD (2017), Income inequality (indicator). doi: 10.1787/459aa7f1-en (Accessed: 21 Nov 2017)

[82] For youth unemployment data: The same source as reference 14

[83] OECD (2017), Poverty rate (indicator). doi: 10.1787/0fe1315d-en (Accessed: 21 Nov 2017)

[84] OECD: OECD Income Distribution Database (IDD): Gini, poverty, income, Methods and Concepts. Available from: http://www.oecd.org/social/income-distribution-database.htm [Accessed:21 Nov 2017]

[85] OECD (2017), Poverty gap (indicator). doi: 10.1787/349eb41b-en (Accessed: 21 Nov 2017)

[86] The same source as reference 85

[87] The same source as reference 7, Exhibit 13

[88] Available from: http://www.ilo.org/global/research/global-reports/weso/2016-transforming-jobs/WCMS_481534/lang--en/index.htm [Accessed: 25 Nov 2017]

[89] Available from: http://www.ilo.org/global/research/global-reports/weso/2017/WCMS_541211/lang--en/index.htm [Accessed: 25 Nov 2017]

[90] The same source as reference 14

[91] Buchan, L. (2017). Britain's debt will not fall to 2008 levels until 2060s, IFS says in startling warning [online]. The Independent. Available from: http://www.independent.co.uk/service/privacy-policy-a6184181.html [Accessed: 25 Nov 2017]

[92] Satisfice. 2017. In Merriam-Webster.com. Available from: https://www.merriam-webster.com/dictionary/satisfice [Accessed: 10 Dec 2017]

[93] Available from the website of Moody's: https://www.moodys.com/Pages/amr002002.aspx?lang=zh-cn&cy=chn [Accessed: 9 Feb 2018]

[94] Available from: https://en.wikipedia.org/wiki/Triple_accreditation. license terms: https://creativecommons.org/licenses/by-sa/3.0/ [Accessed: 9 Feb 2018]

[95] Vogel, P. (2015). Generation Jobless? Turning the youth unemployment crisis into opportunity. Palgrave Macmillan; FutureWork Forum. 2010. Employing the Next Generation. A report by Generation Europe Foundation and The FutureWork Forum

[96] Available online from: https://www.economist.com/news/21732066-why-evangelicals-love-trump-bitcoin-bubble-read-our-selection-stories-download-ten [Accessed: 23 Dec 2017]

[97] Available from the website of Kaizen Institute: https://www.kaizen.com/ [Accessed: 9 Feb 2018]

[98] The same source as reference 55, Figure 9.1

[99] Words were said by Gordon Smith, which Chuck Salter quoted in his article,

Fight to Survive, and this article was published on Fast Company. Available from: The webpage: http://www.fastcompany.com/46314/fight-survive [Accessed: 09 Feb 2018]

[100] Vaillant, G.E. (2013). What are the Secrets to a Happy Life? [online]. Greater Good Magazine. Available from:
https://greatergood.berkeley.edu/article/item/what_are_secrets_to_happy_life [Accessed: 09 Feb 2018]

[101] The World Bank (Sep 2015). FAQs: Global Poverty Line Update. Available from:
http://www.worldbank.org/en/topic/poverty/brief/global-poverty-line-faq [Accessed: 23 Aug 2017]

[102] Bregman, R. (April 2017). Poverty isn't a lack of character; it's a lack of cash [online]. TED. Available from:
https://www.ted.com/talks/rutger_bregman_poverty_isn_t_a_lack_of_character_it_s_a_lack_of_cash#t-12036 [Accessed: 23 Aug 2017]

[103] Proctor et al. (Sep 2016). Income and Poverty in the United States: 2015[online]. United States Census Bureau. Available from:
https://www.census.gov/library/publications/2016/demo/p60-256.html [Accessed: 23 Aug 2017]

[104] The same source as reference 7, page 20

[105] Azoulay,P., Jones,B., Kim,J.D., & Miranda,J. (2018). Research: The Average Age of a Successful Startup Founder Is 45 [online]. Harvard Business Review. Available from: https://hbr.org/2018/07/research-the-average-age-of-a-successful-startup-founder-is-45

[106] BCG Perspectives. Your strategy needs a strategy [online]. Available from: https://www.bcgperspectives.com/yourstrategyneedsastrategy [Accessed: 23 Aug 2017]

[107] Based on information of an article written by feifeima, published on 08 Jan 2017, on feifeima-uk, Weixin

[108] Sherman, E. (Nov 2015). 7 Billionaires Worried about Income Inequality [online]. Available from: http://fortune.com/2015/11/28/billionaires-income-inequality/[Accessed: 23 Aug 2017]

[109] Kiron, D et al. (2017). Corporate sustainability at a crossroads: Progress toward our common future in uncertain times. Summary Findings From the Sustainability Global Executive Studies, 2009-2016 [online]. MIT Sloan Management Review. Available from:
https://sloanreview.mit.edu/projects/corporate-sustainability-at-a-crossroads/ [Accessed: 09 Feb 2018]

[110] Bloom, N. (2017). Corporations in the age of inequality [online]. Harvard Business Review. Available from:
https://hbr.org/cover-story/2017/03/corporations-in-the-age-of-inequality [Accessed: 09 Feb 2018]

[111] Available from: https://en.wikipedia.org/wiki/Up_Series#John. license terms: https://creativecommons.org/licenses/by-sa/3.0/ [Accessed: 09 Feb 2018]

[112] Mankiw, N. G. (2015). Yes, r > g. So What?. American Economic Review: Papers & Proceedings 2015, 105(5): 43–47. http://dx.doi.org/10.1257/aer.p20151059. Available online from: https://scholar.harvard.edu/files/mankiw/files/yes_r_g_so_what.pdf [Accessed: 09 Feb 2018]

www.ingramcontent.com/pod-product-compliance
Lightning Source LLC
Chambersburg PA
CBHW070625220526
45466CB00001B/98